TH
SY

THE JUDAS SYNDROME

Seven Ancient Heresies Return to Betray Christ Anew

By

Thomas Colyandro

Saint Benedict Press
Charlotte, North Carolina

ISBN: 978-1-935302-18-6

Cover design by Tony Pro.

Printed and Bound in the United States of America

SAINT
BENEDICT
PRESS

Saint Benedict Press, LLC
Charlotte, North Carolina
2010

I am the good shepherd; I know my own and my own know me, as the Father knows me and I know the Father; and I lay down my life for the sheep. And I have other sheep, that are not of this fold; I must bring them also, and they will heed my voice. So there shall be one flock, one shepherd. For this reason the Father loves me, because I lay down my life, that I may take it again. No one takes it from me, but I lay it down of my own accord. I have power to lay it down, and I have power to take it again; this charge I have received from my Father.

John 10:14-18

ACKNOWLEDGMENTS

From family, friends and spiritual directors to professors, students and colleagues, I am humbled by the number of people who have supported and encouraged me over the years. Thank you for allowing me to talk, for reading what I have written and for keeping me in your prayers. You are the inheritance of the Divine Wisdom and you have made all the difference in my life.

Regarding the text, I must extend my most sincere appreciation to the entire team at Saint Benedict Press / TAN Books. In particular, I would like to mention Todd Aglialoro for his belief in this project from the beginning and for his constant guidance throughout. I must also offer my deepest gratitude to Dr. Frances Panchok, Professor of Ecclesiastical History, University of St. Thomas School of Theology at St. Mary's Seminary, for continually fostering my passion for history and historical theology.

Finally, I am eternally indebted to the example and writings of the Apostles and Church Fathers. I pray that my humble contribution to the Church is worthy of the paper it is printed on. With deep gratitude, I am your servant in the Most Holy Trinity.

ABOUT THE AUTHOR

Thomas Colyandro holds Master's degrees in theology and divinity from the University of St. Thomas School of Theology at St. Mary's Seminary in Houston, Texas. He has taught theology, spirituality and ecclesiastical history, as well as conducted retreats and facilitated discernment sessions for pastoral councils, school boards, and parish staffs all across Southeast Texas. The author of over sixty articles, Colyandro has held positions with the University of St. Thomas Center for Faith and Culture as well as the University of St. Thomas School of Theology.

TABLE OF CONTENTS

PREFACE

This book is about preserving truth in a world awash in untruth. It is also about the growing desire of the lay faithful to understand Church teaching and to use it in turn as a context for understanding the modern world.

The ideas in *The Judas Syndrome* have come to me over the decade or so that I have worked in parish ministries, including teaching, facilitating discernment sessions and chaplaincy. They have also come to me in my experience as a writer, a corporate public affairs specialist, a student of theology and an avid reader of both history and current events. Throughout these experiences, I learned that most Christians share remarkably similar beliefs about the role faith should play in their lives. They all hope for a closer union with God, desire a more devout prayer life and react positively to historical theology as a means of achieving that increased devotion.

Accordingly, my first hope for this book is that you will gain a greater understanding of the historical development of Church doctrine by becoming more familiar with the debate surrounding certain early heresies such as Arianism (denying Jesus is God), Pelagianism (denying man is dependent on God), and Iconoclasm (denying the use of images of God in prayer). You might think that those heresies have much to do with obscure debates among people long dead and little to do with modern life in the pews. But I believe the controversies over doctrine in the first centuries of the Church strike at the very heart of the challenges we face today.

Therefore, my second hope is that you will be able to make connections between what happened in the early days of the Church and what is happening today: to see how the world is resurrecting ancient heresies and passing them off as modern cultural orthodoxy. Gnosticism-Docetism, for example, is alive in Scientology, in the entertainment world and even some parishes. Pelagianism is rampant in American culture and can be found in modernist spirituality and homiletics. Macedonianism has reappeared in the New Age movement and in modernist spiritualities within the Church. Origenism can be found not only within the wider secularist culture, but also among Christians who dismiss the truth of the final judgment. Because of the reappearance of these heresies and others, there's an urgency in Western Christianity today[1]—to identify them when they occur in your community, at your parish and maybe even in your home. And then, as did our fathers in faith, to defeat them.

---

1. I use "Western Christianity" here because it cannot be denied that Christians in the East must be examined differently due to the brutalities they suffered in the Holy Land and throughout Eastern Europe and Russia.

INTRODUCTION

What is the Judas Syndrome?

The internal life of God is an unknowable mystery; yet we still know God and experience Him too. How is this possible?

First, we exist and God communicates to us. With a love intense and freely given, God created a hierarchy of angelic beings to glorify Him and a hierarchy of ecclesiastical beings (mankind) to serve Him and to join with Him in eternity. By a wisdom deep and all-encompassing, God enlivened our minds and illumined our hearts so that we could receive what He wanted to communicate to us: namely, the gift of Himself.

Secondly, God gathers us together so that we can come to know Him more intimately. God knew that each of us could not grasp Him individually. He knew that we would need to gather together as a body of believers (who would testify to His love for us) under the direction of a body of teachers (who would preserve the Truth for us) in order to understand and share His invitation to union with Him. Therefore, He sent His Son to tell us of the way to redemption and the path toward sanctification—first understood by the prophets, then by the evangelists and the Apostles, and finally preserved by their successors throughout time.

Lastly, God desires our return to Him. He told us from the beginning that His message was meant for every person in every corner of the world. So He created the Church, where ordinary people of all races and nations could see, hear, smell, touch and taste Heaven. He calls us together so that we can catch a glimpse of the life to come and to invite us into a more intimate union with Him now—in preparation for the time to come after our death.

Unfortunately, the free will endowed to man, which allows him to choose to participate in the life God offers to us, has also meant that there are those who choose to reject God and His Church. Man's sinfulness has spilled over into that space where the mind (intellect) meets the heart (spirit) in faith, causing doubt, confusion and scandal among believers of every age. These heretics betrayed Christ no less than Judas Iscariot did, caused the same kind of mayhem Judas caused, and ultimately found their way to the same end Judas found: despair and disgrace. This proud, sinful pattern of betrayal, the *Judas Syndrome*, has plagued Christ's Church since its founding and will continue to plague it until He comes again.

For the rest of us who continue to believe, we must find the strength not only to guard against further degradation of the faith but also to fight against the forces that wish to destroy the Church, just as they did in the first few centuries after Christ. Even though we know all too well that we are unworthy of this call, we must remind ourselves that steadfastness in faith and truth is readily available to us if only we pray for it. This is precisely why we make one last admission of guilt and one last plea for mercy before we go to Holy Communion: we must always remind ourselves not only of the incomprehensible, yet personal, nature of the gift of the transubstantiated bread and wine, but also remember that we need the strength of the Eucharist so as not to do what Judas did.

That is why the believer avows, as put most profoundly in the Byzantine Liturgy of St. John Chrysostom, "Accept me today as a partaker of your mystical supper, O Son of God, for I will not reveal your mystery to your enemies, nor will I give you a kiss as did Judas."

CHAPTER ONE

A Thread of Betrayal

THE MAJOR EVENTS of the gospels were prefigured throughout the Old Testament, and the betrayal of Judas is no exception. For example, in *2 Maccabees* 14, Alcimus, a Hellenized
Jew, tries to destroy the reputation and ultimately seek the death
of Judas Maccabeus, who was credited for the revolt against the
Seleucid Empire and the restoration of Jewish worship in the Jerusalem Temple in 165 BC.

> [Alcimus] answered: "Those of the Jews who are called Haside'ans,
> whose leader is Judas Maccabe'us, are keeping up war and stirring up
> sedition, and will not let the kingdom attain tranquility. Therefore I
> have laid aside my ancestral glory—I mean the high priesthood—
> and have now come here, first because I am genuinely concerned
> for the interests of the king, and second because I have regard also
> for my fellow citizens. For through the folly of those whom I have
> mentioned our whole nation is now in no small misfortune. Since
> you are acquainted, O king, with the details of this matter, deign to
> take thought for our country and our hard-pressed nation with the
> gracious kindness which you show to all. For as long as Judas lives, it
> is impossible for the government to find peace."[1]

In this passage, Alcimus, a high priest, tries to convince the king
of the Seleucid Empire that Judas Maccabeus is a traitor to the

---

1. *2 Mach.* 14:6-10.

crown and to the people when, in fact, the opposite is true. In other words, Alcimus was a deceitful liar who, in seeking ever-greater closeness with the king, conspired to eliminate the truly righteous, God-loving Judas from a place of honor among the Jews. Alcimus's attempt to hand over Judas Maccabeus is not very different than what Judas Iscariot did to Jesus.

Elsewhere in the Old Testament, King David is likewise betrayed by his family members, friends and counselors. *2 Samuel* 15:12 explains: "And while Ab'salom was offering the sacrifices, he sent for Ahith'ophel the Gi'lonite, David's counselor, from his city Giloh. And the conspiracy grew strong, and the people with Ab'salom kept increasing." Upon hearing of the effort against the kingdom, David gathers his officials, who respond with loyalty and bravery in verse 17:15: "And the king's servants said to the king, 'Behold, your servants are ready to do whatever my lord the king decides.'" Finally, in 17:23: "When Ahith'ophel saw that his counsel was not followed, he saddled his ass, and went off home to his own city. And he set his house in order, and hanged himself; and he died, and was buried in the tomb of his father."

The trajectory of this Old Testament story parallels what happened between Jesus and Judas: a close friend and counselor sought his own selfish human ends, betrayed his virtuous king, became disgraced and hanged himself. David laments these betrayals in the *Psalms*—41:9 is particularly important because this is a recollection where David is saddened by the fact that it was a close confidant who deceived him. "Even my bosom friend in whom I trusted, who ate of my bread, has lifted his heel against me." This is striking in that it parallels what Judas had done, not only while he was working for the Twelve (recall that Judas was in charge of the common purse), but also in the midst of breaking bread with Christ. This experience of the betrayal of David comes up again in *Psalm* 55:13-14: "But it is you, my equal, my companion, my familiar friend. We used to hold sweet converse together; within God's house we walked in fellowship."

There are other striking similarities in the Old Testament where the betrayal of Jesus is prophesied. For example, the thirty pieces of silver that Judas received is a reference to the thirty pieces paid for a slave in *Exodus* 21:32, and noted again in *Zechariah* 11:12: "And they weighed out as my wages thirty shekels of silver." Finally, Isaiah prophesies the betrayal of Jesus in 28:1: "Woe to the proud crown of the drunkards of E'phraim, and to the fading flower of its glorious beauty, which is on the head of the rich valley of those overcome with wine!" This is important because the crown refers to the arrogance of the Sanhedrin, and the drunkards refer to Judas because he was a descendent of Ephraim.

These Old Testament passages form the bridge that links the betrayals by Lucifer the fallen angel, the serpent in the Garden of Eden, of Adam and Eve to Judas, the early heretics and beyond. In each case, the betrayers exhibited the Judas Syndrome because they betrayed God from within the community of people through which God chose to reveal Himself. By seeking position, profit and power (man's ends) over salvation (God's ends), these deceitful souls sought to serve themselves because they could not stand to serve God.

• The Story of Judas

Although he shared with the other eleven Apostles a bond around the desire for truth and closeness with God, Judas remained a little too earthly, keeping his eyes on a possible alternative plan just in case life with Jesus didn't work out.

And when it was evening he came with the twelve. And as they were at table eating, Jesus said, "Truly, I say to you, one of you will betray me, one who is eating with me." They began to be sorrowful, and to say to Him one after another, "Is it I?" He said to them, "It is one of the twelve, one who is dipping bread in the same dish with me. For the Son of man goes as it is written of Him, but woe to that man by whom the Son of man is betrayed! It would have been better for that man if he had not been born."[2]

Woe, indeed, to those who at first proclaim Jesus as Lord, then betray him for political purposes! Worse still is the man who would do such a thing for a pittance, the price of a slave. That is the difference between the above passage and the same one that appears in *Matthew 26*, where Judas has made already made his deal with the chief priests. The Gospel of *Luke* expresses the same event, too, but the difference there is that Luke identifies that it was *evil* that had entered Judas as he conspired with the chief priests to arrest Jesus.

Now the feast of Unleavened Bread drew near, which is called the Passover. And the scribes were seeking how to put Him to death; for they feared the people. The Satan entered into Judas called Iscariot, who was of the number of the twelve; he went away and conferred with the chief priests and captains how he might betray Him to them. And they were glad, and engaged to give him money. So he agreed, and sought an opportunity to betray Him to them in the absence of the multitude.[3]

Take note of the sense of the growing tension in Judas. At one level, Judas is just being a sinner: acting selfishly and greedily. At another level, Judas is allowing evil to overtake him, increasing in bitterness and anger towards God.

---

2. *Mark* 14:17-21.
3. *Luke* 22:1-3.

The phenomenally interesting twist in the Gospel of *John* is that Satan enters Judas *right after he receives the bread of life from Jesus.*

When Jesus had thus spoken, He was troubled in spirit, and testified, "Truly, truly, I say to you, one of you will betray me." The disciples looked at one another, uncertain of whom He spoke. One of His disciples, whom Jesus loved, was lying close to the breast of Jesus; so Simon Peter beckoned to him and said, "Tell us who it is of who He speaks." So lying thus, close to the breast of Jesus, he said to him, "Lord, who is it?." Jesus answered, It is he to whom I shall give this morsel when I have dipped it." So when He had dipped the morsel, He gave it to Judas, the son of Simon Iscariot. Then after the morsel, Satan entered into him. Jesus said to him, "What you are going to do, do quickly." Now no one at the table knew why He said this to him. Some thought that, because Judas had the money box, Jesus was telling him, "Buy what we need for the feast"; or, that he should give something to the poor. So, after receiving the morsel, he immediately went out; and it was night.[4]

Here again, the gospel accounts move from expressing Judas's betrayal first as a function of his desire for sociopolitical gain, then about his intimacy with the other eleven Apostles (Judas betrays Jesus immediately prior to the institution of the Eucharist), and finally concerning his intimacy with Jesus (after he had eaten the bread given to him by Jesus). This same arc of betrayal is what is found in the Old Testament.

Having witnessed this act of betrayal, then, it was vital for the Apostles in the earliest Church—and remains acutely relevant for their successors, the bishops, today—to be able to preserve

---

4. *John* 13:21-30.

and protect the truths Jesus revealed. After the Resurrection and Ascension—and especially after the Pentecost—the job of the Apostles was to tend to their flock of believers and to evangelize the nonbelievers. Woven into that mission was their understanding that they were acting on His behalf through the power of the Holy Spirit so that every believer in every age could experience Jesus directly as well. That is why Jesus told them, "Go therefore and make disciples of all nations, baptizing them in the name of the Father and of the Son and of the Holy Spirit, teaching them to observe all that I have commanded you; and lo, I am with you always to the close of the age."[5]

Continually calling His flock to Himself, Jesus also commands us to partake of Him: "And He took bread, and when He had given thanks He broke it and gave it to them, saying, 'This is my body which is given for you. Do this in remembrance of me.'"[6]

• ANCIENT HERESIES AND MODERN TIMES

Looking at our salvation history with an eye towards the Judas Syndrome presents us with the striking dichotomy of a people who seek the light that comes from true light and the substance that comes from real substance—over and against a people who are disgraced before God because they seek their own ends.

What this means is that understanding the great historical heresies such as Gnosticism-Docetism, Origenism, Arianism, Macedonianism, Pelagianism, Iconoclasm, and Messalianism not as the mere ravings of hermitic lunatics, but as *betrayals* of God and His Church, is an important key to unlocking the rather confusing and disheartening times in which we live. Learning to root

---

5. *Matt.* 28:19-20.
6. *Luke* 22:19.

out such betrayals when we encounter them today will strengthen Christ's Church and will illuminate us with the divine love and wisdom that has been bestowed on us and that urgently ushers us toward our ultimate goal: *theosis* or union with God for all eternity.

CHAPTER TWO

Gnosticism/Docetism
Denying the Body of Christ

G OD NEVER INTENDED to remain distant from man. Even though the internal life of God (His essence) is truly un-knowable by human activity alone, we are able to know God by His external life (His energies or grace). How? God chose to allow His superabundant love and His supernatural wisdom to emanate so as to create the celestial, ecclesiastical[1] and natural hierarchies. In so doing, God was communicating to us that He hoped and expected our eventual, eternal return to Him. Therefore, between the time of our own specific creation and our return to Him in death, God gives us Himself, not only in spirit, but in the flesh of Jesus Christ, so that we might find our way through life to Him. In other words, God always intended to manifest Himself to us *physically* so that we might understand how to know Him, love Him and serve Him as we await our eternal life in Heaven.

There have been some throughout history who could not accept the idea that God is so intimate with mankind that He would enter the world Himself in the flesh. The Gnostics and Docetists were guilty of this heresy, rejecting the goodness of flesh for man-kind and the possibility that a true god could be embodied in that same flesh.

---

1. According to Pseudo-Dionysius, St. Maximos and others, this is the natural order of mankind.

Today, Scientologists are a quintessentially Gnostic sect in that they specifically reject bodily existence, claiming that man's treasure is in his "spirit" and rejecting the idea that God could come in the form of a human person. Gnostic and Docetistic thinking can also be found in the entertainment industry, for example, in science fiction and fantasy movies where the main characters are endowed with the ability to know or to learn something that no one else can know. These characters have a specialized *gnosis* (knowledge) about what will "save" them or all mankind without also relying on divine revelation. Finally, certain types of Gnostic thinking can be found in modernist spiritualities, largely influenced by non-Christian Eastern religions, that reject the need for specificity in spiritual reflection.

This means that there has been an avalanche of Christian "spiritualities" and spiritual reflection tools over the last four decades that don't require the user to reflect on the Body of Christ, whether in terms of His humanity or His gift of the Eucharist. These so-called systems of wisdom and reflection ignore the key element of Christian faith: God became man so that man could become more like God (to paraphrase St. Athanasius). We know this is true not only because Jesus the Christ walked the earth, but also because God was revealing Himself to our forefathers in the faith *before* the Incarnation.

- God was Beginning to Reveal the Body of Christ in the Old Testament

Almost immediately after creation, God began to reveal Himself to mankind. In word, image and deed, God wanted us to know who He is so that we might be comforted in our afflictions, so that He might reprove us for our unbelief and inaction, and so that we

might know how to return to Him. This can be seen clearly in the
Old Testament, starting with Abraham.

> And the Lord appeared to him by the oaks of Mamre, as he sat at
> the door of his tent in the heat of the day. He lifted up his eyes and
> looked, and behold, three men stood in front of him. When he saw
> them, he ran from the tent door to meet them, and bowed himself
> to the earth, and said, "My lord, if I have found favor in your sight,
> do not pass by your servant. Let a little water be brought, and wash
> your feet, and rest yourselves under the tree, while I fetch a morsel of
> bread, that you may refresh yourselves, and after that you may pass
> on—since you have come to your servant." So they said, "Do as you
> have said."[2]

Take note of the Trinitarian character of Abraham's experience
of God in the above passage. Already, the first true patriarch was
coming to know something of the personhood of a God who desired to reach out so that we might really care about Him and
about our relationship with Him. In modeling His intimate and
personal care for us, we began to know how to become intimate
with God (and hospitable too!).

In contrast to the experience of Abraham, God chose to reveal Himself to Moses as the most holy God before whom every
knee must bend. The experience of Moses in front of the burning
bush was in some ways an affirmation of the existence and inef-
fability of God. In other words, the Abraham experience was so
very immanent whereas the initial Moses experience was so very
transcendent. Thus, at a personal level, God showed us that it was
good to be intimate with Him—but never to forget how to revere
Him.

---

2. *Gen.* 18:1-5

And the angel of the Lord appeared to him in a flame of fire out of the midst of a bush; and he looked and lo, the bush was burning, yet it was not consumed. And Moses said, "I will turn aside and see this great sight, why the bush is not burnt." When the Lord saw that he turned aside to see, God called to him out of the bush, 'Moses, Moses'! And he said, "Here am I." Then He said, "Do not come near; put off your shoes from your feet, for the place on which you are standing is holy ground." And He said, "I am the God of your father, the God of Abraham, the God of Isaac, and the God of Jacob." And Moses hid his face, for he was afraid to look at God.[3]

It should be noted that, in the two passages above, God's people are beginning to learn how to worship Him. In the case of Abraham, we are taught to act out the living sacrifice, and in the case of Moses, we are taught to approach His altar with a kind of fear and trembling. These two actions take place in every liturgy to this day.

God also revealed Himself at the communal level so that we might know that He has a plan for us. God spoke to the Jewish people and made a covenant with them, which meant that God wanted the world to know that He loved us and is active and present in the communities man creates. In personally looking after His flock, God protected the Jewish nation as they escaped from Egypt.

And God said to Moses. "I am the Lord. I appeared to Abraham, to Isaac, and to Jacob, as God Almighty, but by my name the Lord I did not make myself known to them. I also established my covenant with them, to give them the land of Canaan, the land in which they dwelt as sojourners. Moreover I have heard the groaning of the people of

---

3. *Ex.* 3:2-6.

Israel whom the Egyptians hold in bondage and I have remembered my covenant. Say therefore to the people of Israel, 'I am the Lord, and I will bring you out from under the burdens of the Egyptians, and I will deliver you from their bondage, and I will redeem you with an outstretched arm and with great acts of judgment, and I will take you for my people, and I will be your God; and you shall know that I am the Lord your God, who has brought you out from under the burdens of the Egyptians. And I will bring you into the land which I swore to give to Abraham, to Isaac, and to Jacob; I will give it to you for a possession. I am the Lord.'"[4]

In continuing to show His love for mankind, God also began to reveal Himself to the prophets of the Old Testament. God *could have* spoken to His people just once and expected us to understand everything He wanted us to know and to do, but God's love is too generous (and His knowledge of human nature too accurate) to allow His people to wander unguided in the desert forever. So, through His prophets, God continued to reveal Himself in manifest ways so that our forefathers could begin to testify to us that He was coming among us.

And when they went, I heard the sound of their wings like the sound of many waters, like the thunder of the Almighty, a sound of tumult like the sound of a host; when they stood still, they let down their wings. And there came a voice from above the firmament over their heads; when they stood still, they let down their wings. And above the firmament over their heads there was the likeness of a throne, in appearance like sapphire; and seated above the likeness as it were of a human form. And upward from what had the appearance of his loins I saw as it were gleaming bronze, like the appearance of fire enclosed

---

4. *Ex.* 6:2-8.

round about; and downward from what had the appearance of his loins I saw as it were the appearance of fire, and there was brightness round about him.[5]

The above passage is a clear, early example of God revealing Himself to Ezekiel in the form of a man. For Christians, the man is Christ, and if you take the time to combine the Ezekiel passage with what is being written in the wisdom books of the Old Testament, the revelation of God-as-man is even stronger. In the book of *Sirach*, for example, it is revealed that not only is God coming among us as a man but that we should prepare a tent or tabernacle for Him.

Then the Creator of all things gave me a commandment, and the one who created me assigned a place for my tent. And he said, "Make your dwelling in Jacob, and in Israel receive your inheritance." From eternity, in the beginning, he created me, and for eternity I shall not cease to exist. In the holy tabernacle I ministered to him, and so I was established in Zion. In the beloved city likewise he gave me a resting place, and in Jerusalem was my dominion. So I took root in an honored people, in the portion of the Lord, who is their inheritance.[6]

Notice the structural connections in these four Old Testament passages. God reveals Himself to mankind as three persons so that we might recline with Him in hospitality, but He also makes us shade our eyes as He reveals Himself in His heavenly glory. Then, in *Ezekiel* and *Sirach,* God reveals His face and requires of us a tabernacle. The above Old Testament texts are examples of prefigurations of the Incarnation and the institution of the Eucharist. God was foretelling that His plan was to come among us

---

5. *Ezech.* 1:24-27.
6. *Sirach* 24:8-12.

in *bodily form* in order to prove to us that He created, redeemed and continually sanctifies us until we return to Him.

- ## THE REVELATION OF THE BODY OF CHRIST IN THE NEW TESTAMENT

With these prophetic messages, then, it seems almost impossible that so many were so capable of ignoring the Annunciation and denying the birth of God.

> And the angel said to her, "Do not be afraid, Mary, for you have found favor with God. And behold, you will conceive in your womb and bear a son, and you shall call his name Jesus. He will be great, and will be called the Son of the Most High; and the Lord God will give to Him the throne of David, and He will reign over the house of Jacob for ever; and of His kingdom there will be no end." . . . And while they were there, the time came for her to be delivered. And she gave birth to her first-born son and wrapped him in swaddling cloths, and laid Him in a manger, because there was no place for them in the inn.[7]

It might be understandable, perhaps, that as broken and sinful humans, those who existed before the time of Christ and at the time Mary conceived could not understand what God had done in making the Word become flesh so that we might behold "His glory, glory as of the only Son from the Father."[8] Perhaps those people were not quite ready to accept that the Holy Spirit was working in them as the person and the mechanism by which God would make it so that they might know God-in-Jesus personally.

---

7. *Luke* 1:30-33, 2:6-7.
8. *John* 1:14.

Sadly, there is also the great possibility that some of those people purposefully chose not to believe that God walked among them and that upon Jesus the power of creation rested. Thus, as Jesus walked the earth, He was compelled by love not only to teach but also to perform miracles so that people could come to know God. Keep in mind that God's desire to help people know Him is not exclusive of the miracles of generosity, but also of the dangerous work of continually repelling the lies of Satan, who tries to confuse, confound and dissuade God's people from His message. Christ on earth was fighting the devil in addition to man's ignorance and stubbornness.

A great example of this work took place when Jesus—both in His own humanness (meaning that He felt sadness) and in His role as Savior (meaning that He saw a need to reveal Himself to His people)—resuscitated Lazarus from the grips of death. In doing so, Jesus demonstrated His power over evil, and He also testified dramatically that the physical body matters, that it is good.

> Now when Jesus came, He found that Laz'arus had already been in the tomb four days . . . When Martha heard that Jesus was coming, she went and met Him, while Mary sat in the house. Martha said to Jesus, "Lord, if you had been here, my brother would not have died. And even now I know that whatever you ask from God, God will give you." Jesus said to her, "Your brother will rise again." Martha said to Him, "I know that he will rise again in the resurrection at the last day." Jesus said to her, "I am the resurrection and the life; he who believes in me, though he die, yet shall he live, and whoever lives and believes in me shall never die. Do you believe this?"[9]

Through the second person of the Trinity—the Word coming to the world in flesh—we have the means to participate in the life

---

9. *John* 11:17, 20-26.

of God. What is striking here is that Christ did not merely give us His teaching but He gave us *Himself*, His very Body and Blood. This physicality is an enormously important part of who God-as-Jesus was and who He is for us to this day.

> So Jesus said to them, "Truly, truly, I say to you, unless you eat the flesh of the Son of man and drink His blood, you have no life in you; he who eats my flesh and drinks my blood has eternal life, and I will raise him up at the last day. For my flesh is food indeed, and my blood is drink indeed. He who eats my flesh and drinks my blood abides in me, and I in him. As the living Father sent me, and I live because of the Father, so he who eats me will live because of me. This is the bread which came down from heaven, not such as the fathers ate and died; he who eats this bread will live for ever."[10]

• The Gnostic Heresy Rejected the Human Body

Even after all of these materially real activities—the prophecies, the theophanies, the Incarnation, the Institution of the Eucharist, the Crucifixion and the Resurrection—had taken place, many people still did not believe. Too few of them could conceive that God's love was so superabundant that He could choose to make Himself into flesh—even choose to die. Granted, these concepts were seen as radical in a first century with only one monotheistic religion—Judaism, which preached a personal but always distant God. These ideas were also unthinkable to a Gentile world, which was either drenched in pagan mythologies or beholden to a pre-Christian Greek system of philosophy that believed that

---

10. *John* 6:53-58.

the material world is but a poor copy of the ideal world and that the intellectual life is so far superior to the physical life that death would be a welcome release from the limitations of the bodily form.

Within this context grew Gnosticism—from the Greek word *gnostikos,* meaning "good at knowing"—as a conglomeration of ideas and practices that began to coalesce before the time of Christ in Syria and Egypt.[11] Among Gnosticism's various types and manifestations were a few consistent themes: first, that the physical universe was a degraded form of reality that had once existed or still exists in some deified being; secondly and following from the first, that physical matter represented a degraded form of the spirit of a person; thirdly, that the purpose of life was to overcome the degradation of the fleshly world and to return to the spirit world of the spiritual being; and finally, that the soul could attain a type of salvation by acquiring certain knowledge about the universe.

These four central themes were supported by the Gnostic belief in a *demiurge,* a god who created hosts of demigods functioning as pantheistic deities in the heavens and impacting processes on earth. Gnostics were obsessed with numerology, abused the idea of wisdom, and practiced rituals with incoherent incantations (akin to magic and the occult) intended to assist a person in accessing the knowledge so vital to their "salvation." This sect did not believe in sin per se, but a person who lacked the required enlightenment was seen as *sinful* in the sense that his lack of proper knowledge originated from an interior defect of some kind. This same concept was further used to explain that the negative or "sinful" actions of the demigods were responsible for bringing the fallacies of the physical world into existence.

---

11. The antinomian strain of Gnosticism flourished in Asia Minor, and the dualist strain began in Rome and also spread to Asia Minor.

Eventually, Gnosticism borrowed terminology from Christianity and adapted ritual acts to look like the Sacraments of Baptism, Confirmation, and Eucharist. They wrote prodigiously, producing numerous apocryphal gospels attributed to Judas, Peter, Matthias, Philip, Thomas, the Twelve, and the Egyptians, as well as apocryphal books of acts attributed to Peter, Andrew, John and Thomas. They viewed Jesus, not as the God who loves, suffers, offers grace and awaits our union with Him, but as a superhuman bridge between god and mankind that had come into the world without a human nature, in order to teach the world how to develop knowledge of the good god and to show them how to access "true" knowledge.

- ## The Docetist Heresy Rejected the Incarnation

One specific type of "Christian" Gnosticism was Docetism, which received its name from a derivation of the Greek word *dokesis,* meaning appearance or semblance. These Gnostics were termed "Docetists" because they denied the human nature of Christ, teaching that Jesus only *appeared* to have a human form. Even though they accepted the teaching that some type of "savior" would come into the world, as Gnostics, the Docetists could not believe that God would enter the world in His own flesh, let alone the idea that Jesus was that God-in-flesh. These heretics taught variations on this theme, including the theory that Jesus never actually existed; that the savior did come but that he used a body (called Jesus) in order to visit the world; that Jesus' presence was similar to that of the three angels who appeared to Abraham; that Jesus' body was made of different, heavenly material, not the flesh of humans on earth; that Jesus received an altogether different body upon his Baptism; and that Jesus was the savior but not physically born of Mary. Other forms of Docetism denied Jesus' physical suffering and death, while others proposed that Jesus allowed another person, probably Simon of Cyrene, to be His substitute on the Cross.[12]

- ### ST. PAUL AND ST. JOHN ON JESUS: GOD IN FLESH

This attack on the physical reality of the Word of God coming in the flesh is a direct contradiction to the holy orthodox faith as it was handed down to the Church by Jesus Christ and through the Holy Spirit. As Gnosticism, and Docetism in particular, began to grow in the early decades after the life and death of Jesus Christ, St. Paul almost immediately went to work combating them. In the letter to the Colossians from the early 60s, he wrote, "For in Him all the fullness of God was pleased to dwell, and through Him to reconcile to Himself all things, whether on earth or in heaven, making peace by the blood of His cross."[13]

The use of the term "blood" in this passage is a purposeful reference to the physical, human nature of Christ. St. Paul was also writing to us to say that the Father willingly sent the Son in flesh into the world and that in the world He maintained the fullness of the divine nature while taking on a human one. By connecting divinity and humanity in this way, Jesus as God was drawing all things into Himself, making them whole again by the physical acts of crucifixion and death on the Cross.

St. John addressed this same issue again in the decade of the 90s.

That which was from the beginning, which we have heard, which we have seen with our eyes, which we have looked upon and touched with our hands, concerning the word of life—the life was made

---

12. Similarly, Muslims believe that Jesus only appeared to be crucified. See 4:157 in the Qur'an.

13. *Col.* 1:19-20.

manifest, and we saw it, and testify to it, and proclaim to you the eternal life which was with the Father and was made manifest to us—that which we have seen and heard and proclaim also to you, so that you may have fellowship with us; and our fellowship is with the Father and with His Son Jesus Christ.[14]

In making use of terms referring to the human senses, St. John wanted the reader to know that Jesus was really and truly physically present in the world in the same way as any other human. Through the hypostatic union—the joining of the divine and the human in Jesus—the Apostles and disciples experienced not merely a spiritual communion with God but also a material one. This union is an important point not merely as a refutation to Gnosticism but as a further testament to the veracity of the Church's teaching on the Eucharist. For as in the first century the Apostles came to know their Savior in His Body and Blood, so too do we know Him personally in the one communion made of the flesh of Christ. St. John made clear that belief in the Incarnation was an absolute matter of faith and, in his first two epistles, condemned those who did not believe in it.

Beloved, do not believe every spirit, but test the spirits to see whether they are of God; for many false prophets have gone out into the world. By this you know the Spirit of God: every spirit which confesses that Jesus Christ has come in the flesh is of God, and every spirit which does not confess Jesus is not of God. This is the spirit of antichrist, of which you heard that it was coming, and now it is in the world already [. . .][15] For many deceivers have gone out into the world, men who will not acknowledge the coming of Jesus Christ in the flesh; such a one is the deceiver and the antichrist.[16]

---

14. *1 Jn.* 1:1-3.
15. *1 Jn.* 4:1-3.
16. *2 Jn.* 7.

Notice how St. John raised the heresy of not believing in the Incarnation to apostasy. He wanted to be clear that one cannot reduce his experience of God to purely spiritual means because, as the Church Fathers always taught, it is too easy to substitute one's psychological or emotional needs and desires for the true Flesh of Christ.

- STS. IGNATIUS OF ANTIOCH, IRENAEUS, CYRIL OF JERUSALEM AND OTHERS ON GOD BECOMING MAN

During the late first century (not long after the last word of Scripture was written), St. Ignatius of Antioch wrote against these Gnostic sects in his letter to the Trallians:

> And so be deaf when anyone speaks to you apart from Jesus Christ, who was of the race of David, the Son of Mary, who was truly born and ate and drank, who was truly persecuted under Pontius Pilate and was really crucified and died in the sight of those "in heaven and on earth and under the earth." Moreover, He was truly raised from the dead by the power of His Father.[17]

At the dawn of the second century, mainstream Christianity was still largely an underground endeavor, and because of persistent persecution and a rampant infatuation with pagan cults throughout the Roman Empire, Gnosticism and its "Christian" versions continued to infect the margins of the community. In addition to repeatedly quoting Scripture—particularly the eyewitness accounts of those who walked with Jesus—the Church Fathers bolstered their communities by explaining the spiritual and an-

---

17. St. Ignatius of Antioch, *Letter to the Trallians*, chapter 9. *Didascalia et Constitutiones Apostolorum*, Volume 1. (Paderborn: Schoningh, 1905).

thropological necessity of Christ's coming in the flesh. In the second century, St. Irenaeus, Bishop of Lyon, wrote:

> When He became incarnate and was made man, he recapitulated in himself the long history of man, summing up and giving us salvation in order that we might receive again in Christ Jesus what we had lost in Adam, that is, the image and likeness of God.[18]

Here Irenaeus is saying that God had to come in the flesh because he had to make right what had gone wrong in Adam. In other words, not only did God have to repair the fleshly existence of man, but He had to show that the nature we have (body, soul and spirit) is what God intended for us to have. Therefore, we cannot deny the importance of our own flesh, or, by extension, the enfleshment of the Second Person of the Trinity.

Not only did the early Christian writers disagree with and debunk the theology surrounding these ideas, but they worked hard at identifying for believers what material and whose material was faithful to the teaching of the Church. Serapion, for example, who was the Patriarch of Antioch, specifically addressed the Docetistic Gospel of Peter.

> For our part, brethren, we receive Peter and the other apostles as Christ, but the writings which falsely bear their names we reject, as men of experience, knowing that such were not handed down to us. For I myself, when I came among you, imagined that all of you clung to the true faith, and without going through the Gospels put forward by them in the name of Peter, I said: "If this is the only thing

---

18. St. Irenaeus of Lyons, *Adversus Haereses*. Translated by Alexander Roberts and William Rambaut from Ante-Nicene Fathers, Vol. 1. Edited by Alexander Roberts, James Donaldson, and A. Cleveland Coxe. (Buffalo, NY: Christian Literature Publishing Co., 1885), book 3, chapter 18, paragraph 1.

that seemingly causes cautious feelings among you, let it be read." But since I have now learnt, from what has been told me, that their mind was lurking in some hole of heresy, I shall give diligence to come again to you; wherefore, brethren, expect me quickly. But we, brethren, gathering to what kind of heresy Marcianus belonged, were enabled by others to study this very Gospel, that is, by the successors of those who began it, whom we call Docetae (for most of the ideas belong to their teaching)—using the material supplied by them, we were enabled to go through it, and discover that the most part indeed was in accordance with the true teaching of the Savior, but that some things were added, which also we place below for your benefit.[19]

Take note of the specific mention of the Docetists in this passage, as well as the mention of Marcianus, who was a well-known Docetist in his day. It is interesting that Serapion, in the time before the final canon of Scripture was promulgated, was going to allow a kind of Scripture study among his people. But in discovering that the people promoting the study of this certain letter were Docestist, Serapion forbade it. Although much in the so-called gospel of Peter was found to be in accordance with true Christianity, there were things added that made it false and unusable.

For his part, St. Cyril, Bishop of Jerusalem, added to the debate by explaining that God did in fact come to earth as flesh. He uses a device commonly used in Scripture, listing the physical things that Jesus did while here on earth.

Believe then that this Only-begotten Son of God for our sins came down from heaven upon earth, and took upon Him this human

---

19. Eusebius, *Ecclesiastical History*, book 5, chapter 19, paragraph 2. Translated by Arthur Cushman McGiffert from Nicene and Post-Nicene Fathers, Second Series, Vol. 1. Edited by Philip Schaff and Henry Wace. (Buffalo, NY: Christian Literature Publishing Co., 1890).

nature of like passions with us, and was begotten of the Holy Virgin and of the Holy Ghost, and was made Man, not in seeming and mere show, but in truth; nor yet by passing through the Virgin as through a channel; but was of her made truly flesh, and did truly eat as we do, and truly drink as we do. For if the Incarnation was a phantom, salvation is a phantom also. The Christ was of two natures, Man in what was seen, but God in what was not seen; as Man truly eating like us, for He had the like feeling of the flesh with us; but as God feeding the five thousand from the five loaves (*Matt.* 14:17 ff).[20]

Notice too how St. Cyril also explains the connections between the earthly Jesus and the heavenly Christ. Jesus ate because His flesh was hungry, but He fed the five thousand in part because their souls were hungry.

The Docetist apostasy continued after the Ecumenical Councils of Nicea (325) and Constantinople (381), both of which defined and defended the revealed nature of God in Jesus Christ. Although the various Gnostic sects had lost most of their impact during that time, it wasn't until the third and fourth ecumenical councils—Ephesus in 431 and Chalcedon in 451—the movement disappeared as an organized force.

- SCIENTOLOGY ON "SECRET KNOWLEDGE" AND THE DENIAL OF THE IMPORTANCE OF HUMAN FLESH

The best example of what Gnosticism was in the first century can be found in various cults today, such as Scientology. Even an anecdotal review of Scientology's stated beliefs demonstrates clear

---

20. St. Cyril of Jerusalem, Catecheses, No. 4:9. Nicene and Post-Nicene Fathers of the Christian Church. Translated into English with prologomena and explanatory notes under the editorial supervision of Philip Schaff, D.D., LL.D., and Henry Wace, D.D. (New York: Charles Scribner's Sons), 1904.

parallels to Gnosticism. As a pseudo-religious group, it aims to indoctrinate members into a philosophical system with mythological overtones for the beginnings of mankind, its purpose and its end. Scientology teaches that man is a spiritual being: not that he is made for a spiritual life, but that his body is in no way part of his personhood. The group teaches that humans can attain higher levels of awareness and unlimited abilities based on their commitment to unlearning what was previously known and discovering hidden knowledge (which it alone seems to know and which no one else seems to be able to know independently).

Scientology teaches its adherents that humans are made up of a spirit (called a *thetan*), which is the real person, and of the mind, which can be used to control the environment around it. This idea that people have special powers to control the world around them is an attempt to convince people that they do not have to be bound by human limitations or by the divine design. Even more than that, it is a way of convincing people that they do not have to function within the human community. Scientology teaches, indeed, that an individual could operate independently of his body and even of the universe.

Although there are some intriguing parallels between Gnosticism and Scientology in the details of their creation myths, it is more important here to know that Scientology exhibits the Judas Syndrome in re-presenting to the world two major elements of Gnosticism: that man is only a spiritual being and that his "salvation" is dependent on a secret knowledge. These ideas are important to understand because they are a rejection of the human person as he is made. Unsurprisingly, this group rejects the core Christian doctrines of the Incarnation, the Eucharist, the Crucifixion and the Resurrection, and it rejects our belief that the good news of Jesus Christ is for all people, of all times and places. This is a direct contradiction to the revealed faith that God's creation is good and that He intended that we should be made in the flesh. Not to mention, of course, this is in direct contradiction to the idea and practice of the Eucharist as handed down to us by Christ Himself.

Scientologist language leads to misunderstanding and confusion. Its attractive promises about superior knowledge and behavior can lead the unbeliever, the unchurched, the weak and vulnerable, to follow a path of anti-Christian destruction. This is why the Church has steadfastly maintained that a teaching office of the Church exists and that it is vital to the pastoral care of its members. Think about it this way: the apostolic Faith has always rejected the idea that someone had to have a special knowledge from some magical source in order to come to know, love and serve Christ on earth and to spend eternity with Him in Heaven. But if we had not been able to maintain a legitimate succession of bishops—girded by deep faith and a desire for learned testimony—then it would have been possible for heretics to destroy the truth of Christianity. This is precisely why Scripture and Tradition matter, and it is how you and I can know we are living the true faith.

The Church has long been suspicious of claims of privately revealed "new knowledge." Now, this does not mean that private revelation (such as apparitions) can't or doesn't happen, or that some "saint in our midst" can't offer us a new way to look at things. What it does mean is that if a group makes wild claims about God, the Church or mankind, these claims must somehow be faithfully verified before they can be trusted as true. This is how believers can know that they are not being misled by a group of lunatics.

Gnostic presumptions are a common feature among cults throughout the centuries. Take, for instance, the Heaven's Gate group. They believed that our existing bodies are only "vessels" intended to assist us on a journey and that people were supposed to hate this world enough so that they would want to leave it.

Members of this cult committed mass suicide in order to prepare themselves to be taken by space ships to a new world. David Koresh and the Branch Davidians were of a similar mode of thinking. This is why the protection of revelation and the doctrine that flows from it is an important task of every age.

- GNOSTICISM IN ENTERTAINMENT

There are other more commonplace examples of how Gnosticism has entered the world. From Hollywood we have seen myriad science-fiction and fantasy films that have attempted to promote a purely spiritual or intellectual ideal over and against the divinely-created union of spirit and matter in the human person. These have also sought to describe a process by which people will come to a superior existence by uncovering a secret knowledge available only to those worthy of that knowledge.

The *Matrix* trilogy is an excellent example of Gnosticism in film: its main characters are given a chance to achieve a special knowledge about the universe (namely, that it is a virtual-reality illusion run by computers and machines). Because of their enlightenment and by their supernatural physical and mental capabilities, these characters have the chance to free humanity from its ignorance and reliance on outmoded ways of living. These types of movies and books often include scenes about people who reject conventional thinking, especially historically-based theological and spiritual truths that include God's revelation to man. The people involved are portrayed as somehow more pure because they doubt everything and seek a truth that seems never to have been present in the world of tradition and authority. The seeker or seekers stumblingly discover a world-behind-this-world that, if they choose, will release them from the dictates of divine and natural law, of the community and of the one, true Church.

The goal of the journey in this kind of material is normally portrayed as a new kind of freedom—not the freedom that comes from discerning and following the will of God, but a freedom that frees each person from the limits of being responsible to or for anyone or anything. The characters in these works promote a utopian ideology where somehow, without any context from revelation or an adherence to doctrines or people, everyone in their midst spontaneously shares all of their goods because everyone seems to know that the goal of existence is to be freed from the physical. Just like the Docetists—who were also known as illusionists—the fantasy world created by this particular type of storyteller is one where the Incarnation, Crucifixion and Resurrection can be forgotten about as long as the one reading or watching the story can learn to "free" his own mind.

Gnosticism in Theology and Spirituality

Sadly modern Gnosticism is not limited to cults and movies—it has crept into our churches too in the form of modernism, particularly in North America and Western Europe. The views that make up this kind of spirituality can be traced to the intransigent succession of the Protestant Reformation in the sixteenth century, the beginning of the Enlightenment Period in the seventeenth century, the American and French Revolutions in the eighteenth century, and the industrial revolutions of the eighteenth and nineteenth centuries. These events created a festering breeding ground for the rejection of revelation, Tradition and authority. Although not every person involved in these various revolutions rejected God-in-flesh per se, in them can be found the beginnings of the modern movements that seek to destroy the need for the body of Christ, building instead a purely spiritual or intellectual realm.

The goal of this kind of spirituality is to convince people that historical truths should be placed in doubt and that tradition should be treated with suspicion. For example, there are professors of theology, Scripture, ecclesiastical history, and so on, who use the historical-critical method of research, which attempts to distinguish the truth of historical claims by examining the authenticity of documents, examining archaeological evidence, comparing accounts of a situation, and through other means. Although this approach is a reasonable one at first glance, too many so-called professors of theology and Scripture have used it as a license to cast doubt on everything in the Tradition. They begin by saying that they can only believe what is verifiable by some scientific test. Since they cannot possibly confirm every premise or conclusion in Scripture and Tradition—because many of them are matters of faith—these scholars conclude (and convince their students) that truth is a relative thing and that we must only believe what is physically evident.

For example, there had been a trend in schools of theology to spend time focusing on the Gnostic gospels themselves. While it is certainly legitimate to study such documents as an academic exercise, it is hardly appropriate to portray them as a legitimate historical source of information about Christianity, since they are decidedly not Christian. About the time certain professors of theology decided that it was more important to have the respect of their fellow academics over the respect of the Church, it became simultaneously more important to falsely foster a "healthy sense of independent thinking and belief" over and against a healthy sense of faith and truth. The practical effect of this shift created a crisis among the newly-formed priests, deacons and theologians of those days who were thrust into the world with doubts and concerns instead of clarity.[21]

---

21. An iconic example of this theological school of doubt is the Jesus Seminar.

Conjunctively, the dominance of the psycho-therapeutic world-view in spirituality over the last forty years—which itself was partially influenced by Gnostic taints in popular culture—has crept into the confessionals and offices of spiritual directors as well. This worldview has impacted priests in Catholic parishes, where talk of the resurrected Christ drastically overshadows the crucified Jesus. These same parishes seem no longer to display the crucifix, but rather the cross alone or a cross with a resurrected corpus on it. Sadly, these priests don't recognize the impact of dismissing the connection between the Eternal Word, the living Jesus, and the resurrected Christ. Since God calls each of us to union with Him, this praxis of body and soul is exactly where we must live. With a diminished sense of the life of Jesus that can lead believers to over-spiritualize their faith in an emotionally or psychologically driven framework, it is not hard to understand why survey after survey shows a serious lack of belief in the truth that bread and wine are actually transformed into the Body and Blood of Jesus Christ.

We believe that Jesus is the Eternal Word made flesh and resurrected from the dead. We believe too that we were created as we are—body and soul. We believe that these items of faith are available and knowable to all. As such, we proclaim and we teach that, through the Incarnation, the Eucharist, the Crucifixion and the Resurrection, we were and are brought to a higher (and simultaneously deeper) understanding of the God who created, redeemed and sanctified us. That God did not intend to remain distant from man, nor did He intend for man to remain distant from Himself.

CHAPTER THREE

Arianism
Reducing Christ to a Prophet

JESUS IS THE SECOND PERSON of the Trinity, the Son of God, the Eternal Word. He existed before all time, helped to create the world, and was given dominion over it. He appeared to our forefathers in the faith, spoke to the prophets, offered up His flesh as a sacrifice for the entire world and rose from the dead. He sent us the Holy Spirit, gave us the Church, ascended into Heaven and now sits at the right hand of the Father. Jesus for all times and everywhere was and is God.

Arius was a churchman who rejected this revelation. He was the leader of a community in the early Church that chose to accept a pagan understanding of the one god who appointed a superhuman to act as a viceroy over the created universe. To him and his followers, therefore, Jesus was more than human but less than God.

Jehovah's Witnesses are the clearest example today of a group that preaches Jesus as this "almost-god" figure, sometimes implying that He is equal to the Archangel Michael. Unitarian Universalists are another quasi-Christian group that rejects Christ's divinity as Arius did, believing that God has communicated Himself through many spiritual leaders and prophets and that Jesus is just one among those many. Thus, Unitarians might study Buddha as much as they do Jesus. Disturbingly, Arianism can also be found among some Christian groups engaged in interreligious dialogue, so afraid of offending anyone that they downplay the central Christian (and divisive) doctrine of Christ's divinity.

• GOD REVEALING HIMSELF IN THE OLD TESTAMENT

Even though the people of the Old Testament were not ready to accept that God could come in the flesh, God still showed Himself to the world through a host of physical experiences that were offered to help people come to know God and understand how to join their lives to Him.

In presenting Himself to Moses, God told His people that He was the one God that existed from before all time.

> God said to Moses, "I am who I am." And He said, "Say this to the people of Israel, *I am* has sent me to you." God also said to Moses, "Say this to the people of Israel, The Lord, the God of your fathers, the God of Abraham, the God of Isaac, and the God of Jacob, has sent me to you: this is my name for ever, and thus I am to be remembered throughout all generations."[1]

In presenting Himself to Abraham, on the other hand, God told His people that He would forge a covenant with them forever. You see, God explained to Abraham that because of His love for His people, He would give them a homeland and bless them through the ages if they remained in steadfast love and commitment to the One who saved them. This meant, in part, that the Hebrew people would be given a permanent home and an altar upon which they could praise and glorify God throughout the ages.

---

1. *Ex.* 3:14-15.

Abram passed through the land to the place at Shechem, to the oak of Moreh. At that time the Canaanites were in the land. Then the Lord appeared to Abram and said, "To your descendents I will give you this land." So he built there an altar to the Lord, who had appeared to him. Thence he removed to the mountain on the east of Bethel, and pitched his tent, with Bethel on the west and Ai on the east; and there he built an altar to the Lord and called on the name of the Lord.[2]

Take note of the development in these two passages: God is presenting Himself to us in ways that can be described as divine and human. The experience of Moses is somewhat more philosophical in nature. God simply explains that He is the one who "exists": He is the author of all created being. The second passage with Abram gives man a context in which to live for the Lord. In other words, God was also physical in how He interacted with man. In the first instance, there is but a burning bush. In the second instance, there is a whole land where people can build a home.

Once the Jewish people had this home, it stands to reason that, man being man, the Jewish people would come under attack by their neighbors and enemies. But God did not let them down. When these people became the first to believe, it was He who interceded many times on their behalf. He protected them as a father would protect his children. "Thy right hand, O Lord, glorious in power, thy right hand, O Lord, shatters the enemy."[3] Again, there is a sense here that God was being tangibly present in the world on behalf of the people who were dedicated to Him. In fact, just a few short verses later in that same chapter of *Exodus*, the writer expresses in a slightly different manner how God worked

---

2. *Gen.* 12:6-8.
3. *Ex.* 15:6.

wonders in the world—that is to say, engaged in a physical relationship with His people.

> Who is like thee, O Lord, among the gods? Who is like Thee, majestic in holiness, terrible in glorious deeds, doing wonders? Thou didst stretch out thy right hand, the earth swallowed them.[4]

Later, among the Old Testament prophets, the experience of the physical manifestation of God would become more intense and more deeply spiritual. Going beyond a youthful people's exuberance that God had helped them win some battles and overcome the difficulties of their new land, God actually began to reveal the personal nature of the Trinity. In fact, it was Isaiah who saw a human form in God.

> In the year that King Uzzi'ah died, I saw the Lord sitting upon a throne, high and lifted up; and His train filled the temple. Above Him stood the seraphim; each had six wings: with two he covered his face, and with two he covered his feet, and with two he flew. And one called to another and said: "Holy, holy, holy is the Lord of hosts; the whole earth is full of His glory." And the foundations of the thresholds shook at the voice of him who called, and the house was filled with smoke. And I said: "Woe is me! For I am lost; for I am a man of unclean lips, and I dwell in the midst of a people of unclean lips; for my eyes have seen the Kind, the Lord of hosts!"[5]

Isaiah tried to explain what he saw and to communicate how intense it would be for us when we were fully able to see God in flesh. But he wasn't the only one. In fact, God had begun to reveal Himself to the ancient kings as well.

---

4. *Ex.* 15:11-12.
5. *Is.* 6:1-5.

Then Nebuchadnez'zar was astonished and rose up in haste. He said to his counselors, "Did we not cast three men bound into the fire?' He answered the king, "True, O king." He answered, "But I see four men loose, walking in the midst of the fire, and they are not hurt; and the appearance of the fourth is like a son of the gods."[6]

This really couldn't be any clearer. God began revealing the personhood of the Second Person of the Trinity so that different kinds of people would believe and know. He was trying, in this particular case, to teach the king that every nation and every ruler on earth shall bow to the one ruler Jesus Christ.

- ## Jesus as God in the New Testament

We know that Jesus was the God referred to in the earlier Old Testament passages because it was He who fulfilled what had been revealed to the Fathers and Prophets. Furthermore, it was Jesus who was able to accomplish divine things through a human form. For example, Jesus warned people about not doing the will of His Father. He controlled nature, performed miracles, resuscitated the dead, saw into the hearts of people and drove out demons. In other words, Jesus as God revealed Himself to be physically involved in the world while at the same time revealing Himself as the One who sits on the throne of glory. Since that time we have joyfully become bound by love and wisdom to worship Him, for "he who swears by heaven, swears by the throne of God and by Him who sits upon it."[7]

Jesus was and is more than the prophets, and His followers testified to the world that God had come into its midst.

---

6. *Dan.* 3:69-70.
7. *Matt.* 23:22.

And after six days Jesus took with him Peter and James and John his brother, and led them up a high mountain apart. And he was transfigured before them, and His face shone like the sun, and His garments became white as light. And behold, there appeared to them Moses and Eli'jah, talking with Him. And Peter said to Jesus, "Lord, it is well that we are here; if you wish, I will make three booths here, one for you and one for Moses and Eli'jah." He was still speaking, when lo, a bright cloud overshadowed them, and a voice from the cloud said, "This is my beloved Son, with whom I am well pleased; listen to Him." When the disciples heard this, they fell on their faces, and were filled with awe.[8]

The experience of the transfiguration had served as further proof to the Apostles, specifically Peter, James and John, that the live human person of Jesus was also God. Jesus further testifies to this Himself, saying, "I and the Father are one."[9] Jesus' claim of being the Son of God is the reason that the Sanhedrin wanted to punish Him. They could not bring themselves to believe that the one, transcendent God would become mere human flesh. "This was why the Jews sought all the more to kill Him, because He not only broke the Sabbath but also called God His Father, making Himself equal with God."[10] At the demand of the Jewish people and under the sociopolitical pressures of the Roman Empire, when they had humiliated Jesus, beaten Him, forced Him up the hill at Calvary and nailed Him to the Cross, Jesus did not relent.

When Jesus had spoken these words, He lifted up His eyes to heaven and said, "Father, the hour has come; glorify thy Son that the Son may glorify thee, since thou hast given Him power over all flesh, to

---

8. *Matt.* 17:1-6.
9. *John* 10:30.
10. *John* 5:18.

give eternal life to all whom thou hast given Him. And this is eternal life, that they know thee the only true God, and Jesus Christ whom thou hast sent. I glorified thee on earth, having accomplished the work which thou gavest me to do; and now, Father, glorify thou me in thy own presence with the glory which I had with thee before the world was made."[11]

Those who followed Jesus when He was in the flesh began to understand that He was God, and they tried to explain this to their fellow men, but many did not accept it. Even those who did originally understand—eventually becoming Christians, even serving as priests—were swayed into the darkness. As types of Judas, there were those who tried to explain away the physicality of God or the divinity of Jesus and promote a doctrine that He was some kind of superhuman, more than man but less than God.

- ### ARIUS DID NOT BELIEVE JESUS WAS GOD, MERELY THE HIGHEST HUMAN BEING

Arius was just such a priest; a restless Egyptian churchman who had taken increasingly schismatic positions and by 318 A.D. had finally run afoul of his bishop, Alexander. Arius argued that Jesus was not of the same substance as the Father. He explained that he could not personally reconcile the suffering of the crucifixion with an idea of God who is beyond all things, especially pain and death. In a famous formulation, Arius proposed that Jesus could not be consubstantial with the Father because He was born into humanity and took on a human form. He was capable of believing that Jesus was above all humans, he wrote, but not God Himself.

The ideas of Arius grew in popularity, starting in North Africa

---

11. *John* 17:1-5.

and spreading to Syria, but they were eventually condemned in 321 at a local synod in Alexandria. Arius fled to Palestine after having been excommunicated and began speaking and writing extensively to explain his position to any church leaders who would listen. In 325, he went to Nicea to present to that first ecumenical council a creed he developed, but he was summarily anathematized by the more than three hundred bishops present. That council codified the Christian belief that Jesus is the Son of God and that He shares the same substance of the Father. Out of this controversy came the Nicene Creed, which is the symbol of faith to this day.

Through the acts of the council, Arius was banished to Illyricum, where he encouraged his followers to team up with a group of believers who had sided with an earlier heretic named Meletius in North Africa, and he also began setting up a hierarchy of his own in Alexandria to rival that of the Church. The Emperor Constantine, who knew Arius, asked if there was a way he could be restored to the Church, but St. Athanasius, now bishop of Alexandria, would not allow it. Arius died in 336, but the controversy that he sparked continued for some time after.

• STS. PAUL AND JOHN ON JESUS AS GOD REVEALED

Those who knew Jesus knew that He was the fulfillment of the Old Testament because He was already revealing Himself before being manifested in the flesh. This is what the writer from the community surrounding St. Paul explained to us in the Book of *Hebrews.*

> In many and various ways God spoke of old to our fathers by the prophets; but in these last days He has spoken to us by a Son, whom He appointed the heir of all things, through whom also He created

the world. He reflects the glory of God and bears the very stamp of His nature, upholding the universe by His word of power. When He had made purification for sins, He sat down at the right hand of Majesty on high, having become as much superior to angels as the name He has obtained is more excellent than theirs.[12]

In addition, those who knew Jesus (or at least knew those who knew Him) were also inspired by the Holy Spirit to explain the theological reality of how this man, born of the flesh, was not merely a superhuman but actually shared the substance of the Divine. The Gospel according to St. John, the beloved disciple, is an excellent example of how churchmen were beginning to work out the implications of the revelation that Jesus was more than a man.

In the beginning was the Word, and the Word was with God, and the Word was God. He was in the beginning with God; all things were made through him, and without Him was not anything made that was made. In Him was life, and the life was the light of men. The light shines in the darkness, and the darkness has not overcome it.[13]

John's theological writings are legendary and serve as our standard in the fight against the forces of betrayal at work in Judas, Arius and others.

- Sts. Athanasius, John Chrysostom and Basil the Great on Jesus as God

St. Athanasius, who lived from 293 to 373, spent most of his life fighting against the Arians and is considered one of the great

---

12. *Heb.* 1:1-4.
13. *John* 1:1-5.

Doctors of the Church both in the East and in the West. His famed *Four Orations Against the Arians* was instrumental in combating this heresy in the decades that followed the Council of Nicea in 325, where he was already considered an expert in theology in general and especially on the matter of Jesus' divinity. In defense of the definition promulgated at Nicea, he wrote:

> This then being the force of such titles, in like manner let a man call God unoriginated, if it so please him; not however as if the Word were of originated things, but because, as I said before, God not only is not originated, but through His proper Word is He the maker of things which are so. For though the Father be called such, still the Word is the Father's Image, and one in essence with Him; and being His Image, He must be distinct from things originated, and from everything; for whose Image He is, His property and likeness He has; so that he who calls the Father unoriginated and almighty perceives in the Unoriginated and the Almighty, His Word and His Wisdom, which is the Son.[14]

The basic and complex point Athanasius is making in this passage is that if one were to give God (as Father) the title of "unoriginated" (meaning both that He existed before all time and also that there was no other being that created Him), then it is necessary to give such a title to Jesus, the Son of God, because it is not possible to separate the word of God from God Himself, nor is it possible to separate the wisdom of God from God Himself. Therefore, since we know and believe that Jesus is the Word and Wisdom of God, He has been God from before all time.

---

14. Defense of the Nicene Definition, No. 30, p. 171. *Nicene and Post-Nicene Fathers of the Christian Church*, volume 4. Translated into English with Prologomena and Explanatory Notes under the Editorial Supervision of Philip Schaff, D.D., LL.D., and Henry Wace, D.D. New York, Charles Scribner's Sons, 1904.

For, though no works had been created, still "the Word" of God "was," and "the word was God." And His becoming man would not have taken place, had not the need of men become a cause. The Son then is not a creature. For had He been a creature, He would not have said, "He begets me," for the creatures are from outside, and are works of the Maker; but the Offspring is not from outside nor a work, but from the Father, and proper to His Essence. Wherefore they are creatures; this God's Word and Only-begotten Son.[15]

In this passage, Athanasius distinguishes between what it means to be begotten and what it means to be created. He further explains that Jesus is different from other creatures because He is the One who can create on His own and in so doing create them from His Image. Creatures, however, must rely on a prior cause— God—to create something ourselves.

For none of the things which are brought to be is an efficient cause, but all things were made through the Word: who would not have wrought all things, were He Himself in the number of creatures. For neither would the Angels be able to frame, since they too are creatures, though Valentinus, and Marcion, and Basilides think so, and you are their copyists.[16]

It is rather interesting here that Athanasius was writing against both the Gnostics (mentioning some of them by name) and the

---

15. Four Discourses Against the Arians, No. 2:56. *Nicene and Post-Nicene Fathers of the Christian Church*, vol. IV. Translated into English with Prologomena and Explanatory Notes under the Editorial Supervision of Philip Schaff, D.D., LL.D., and Henry Wace, D.D. New York, Charles Scribner's Sons, 1904), p. 378.

16. Four Discourses Against the Arians, No. 2:21. *Nicene and Post-Nicene Fathers of the Christian Church*, vol. IV. Translated into English with Prologomena and Explanatory Notes under the Editorial Supervision of Philip Schaff, D.D., LL.D., and Henry Wace, D.D. New York, Charles Scribner's Sons, 1904), p. 359.

Arians. As was stated before, the work he did for the Church in this matter was vital in the fourth century as well as for us today.

St. John Chrysostom lived from 347 to 407, was a hermit who became archbishop of Constantinople, developed the most commonly-used Byzantine liturgy (still in use today) and is considered one of the great saints of the Church. He too dealt with the Arian controversy, which had a serious practical impact in the East, where Christians literally had to choose whether or not to follow a separate, Arian hierarchy of bishops and priests. Even though the Council of Nicea had taken place more than twenty years before he was born, the theological and spiritual aftershocks of the Arian controversy were still being felt in Antioch (where Chrysostom lived for most of his life), which is why he saw the need to continue defending and promoting the doctrine of the divinity of Jesus. An additional side effect of the controversy was a growing tension regarding the ecclesiastical supremacy of Constantinople over Alexandria.

One of the better examples of Chrysostom's discourses on Christ comes from his homily on the Gospel of John. Here he focuses on explaining the co-eternity and consubstantiality of Jesus as Son and God as Father:

> Tell me, then, does the radiance of the sun proceed from the substance itself of the sun, or from some other source? Any one not deprived of his very senses needs/must confess, that it proceeds from the substance itself. Yet, although the radiance proceeds from the sun itself, we cannot say that it is later in point of time than the substance of that body, since the sun has never appeared without its rays. Now if in the case of these visible and sensible bodies there has been shown to be something which proceeds from something else, and yet is not after that from whence it proceeds; why are you incredulous in the case of the invisible and ineffable Nature? This same thing

there takes place, but in a manner suitable to That Substance. For it is this reason that Paul too calls him "Brightness" [*Heb.* 1:3]; setting forth thereby His being from Him and His Coeternity. Again, tell me, were not all the ages, and every interval created by Him? Any man not deprived of his sense must necessarily confess this. There is no interval therefore between the Son and the Father; and if there be none, then He is not after, but Co-eternal with him. For 'before' and 'after' are notions implying time, since, without age or time, no man could possibly imagine these words; but God is above times and ages.[17]

His use of the sun and its rays as a metaphor for how the Son is related to the Father was an excellent pedagogical device. The listener would have been able to draw a mental picture and understand Jesus as the radiance of the sun and the Father as the sun, each of the same actual substance. Chrysostom spoke of Jesus as "equal to the Father" and "equal in essence." He begged the community not to fall prey to the lovers of false doctrine. Instead, he exhorted them to remember that God gave Himself as a gift to mankind so that man could become more like God.

St. Basil the Great also defended the Church against Arianism. He lived from 330 to 379 and was the bishop of Caesarea Mazaca in Cappadocia. Basil had a greater impact on the field of Christology than did Chrysostom, as he focused on both the unity (*ousia*) and the distinctiveness of the persons of the Trinity (*hypostasis*).[18]

---

17. Philip Schaff, D.D., L.L.D., ed, *Chrysostom: Homilies on St. John and Hebrews*, vol. XIV of *A Select Library of the Nicene and Post-Nicene Fathers of the Christian Church First Series* (New York: Charles Scribner's Sons, 1904), 17.

18. St. Basil's Trinitarian terminology became the basis for the Council of Chalcedon in 451.

It is indispensable to have a clear understanding that, as he who fails to confess the community of the essence or substance falls into polytheism, so he who refuses to grant the distinction of the *hypostases* is carried away into Judaism. For we must keep our mind stayed, so to say, on a certain underlying subject matter, and, by forming a clear impression of its distinguishing lines, so to arrive at the end desired.[19]

Basil made the important distinction that one must properly understand that the persons of the Trinity share the same substance—the divine substance—because if this is not properly understood then it would be easy to slip into a kind of polytheism. On the other hand, Basil made it clear that one must properly understand the distinction within the Trinity (i.e. the functions of each of the persons) because if this is not properly understood then it would be easy to slip into a kind of modalism where God simply puts on different masks to act and to communicate. Using the language of monarchy, Basil tried to make clear for the Christian community that we believe in the distinctiveness of the person of Christ (*hypostasis*) while still believing in one God (*ousia*).

We speak of a king, and of the king's image, and not of two kings. The majesty is not cloven in two, nor the glory divided. The sovereignty and authority over us is one, and so the doxology ascribed by us is not plural but one; because the honor paid to the image passes on to the prototype. Now what in the one case the image is by reason of imitation, that in the other case the Son is by nature.[20]

---

19. Epistle 210. Philip Schaff, D.D., L.L.D., and Henry Wace, D.D., *eds*, *Basil*, vol. V of *A Select Library of the Nicene and Post-Nicene Fathers of the Christian Church Second Series* (Grand Rapids, Michigan: WM B Eerdmans Publishing, 1904).

20. Philip Schaff, D.D., L.L.D., *ed*, *Basil: Holy Spirit*, vol. VIII of *A Select Library of the Nicene and Post-Nicene Fathers of the Christian Church Second Series* (New York: Charles Scribner's Sons, reprinted 1904), 28.

For Basil, God had to become flesh in order that Jesus might suffer by the flesh, and in so doing, redeem humanity. God the Son paid the price for our sin and destroyed the eternal power of death. If He had not acted in his specific identity, then not only would we not have known our God in such an intimate way, but humanity would have remained forever broken by the sin of Adam. As three of the great early Church fathers from the East, St. Athanasius, St. John Chrysostom and St. Basil the Great, defined and explained elements of Christological and Trinitarian dogma, they each beat back the Arian controversy in ways that are instructive for us as we face those who today—because of the Judas Syndrome—deny the all-important doctrine of Christ's divinity.

- ### Jehovah's Witnesses Deny Jesus is God

The Jehovah's Witnesses were founded in the nineteenth century but evolved into their modern form sometime in the 1930s. Maybe best known for their incessant and intrusive evangelization techniques, Jehovah's Witnesses are also notorious for their belief that Satan has entered the world and that Armageddon is imminent (although they do not make predictions anymore about the date of the end of the world as they mistakenly did in 1914, 1925 and 1975) and for their preaching of a coming eternal paradise on earth, over which precisely 144,000 people will be raised to Heaven in order to rule with Jesus.

Jehovah's Witnesses also specifically teach that Jesus was the first *creation* of God and that all other creatures were made through Him. The group teaches that Jesus died to atone for our sins, that he came to establish His literal kingdom on earth, and that some of the biblical references to the archangels also refer to Jesus—meaning that Jesus may have had some kind of preexistence as a spiritual being, but not as God.

The rejection of the Trinity and the reduction of Christ to a superhuman or angel who is not consubstantial with the Father is a clear reappearance of the old seductive Arian error. It is fortunate, maybe, that Jehovah's Witnesses are considered to live at the margins of reasonable belief and activity. (They reject blood transfusions, military service, national holidays, and religious observances like Easter and Christmas.) But it is not wise to ignore the Jehovah's Witnesses as a marginalized cult remaining to themselves in their "kingdom halls"—rather we must recognize how they prey on the poor, uneducated and unchurched.

 · UNITARIANS VIEW JESUS AS A GREAT EXAMPLE

A second example of how Arianism survives in the world today can be found among the Unitarians. As an originally Protestant sect emerging in France in the eighteenth century, this group adheres to a philosophy that rejects the Trinity and the Divinity of Christ. While members of this group can believe in the teachings of Jesus in the New Testament, more often than not they see Jesus merely as a great example, a moral authority, and even a prophet, but not the Son of God. As such, they also embrace religious pluralism, trying to find equal value in all religious traditions.

The Protestant-based Unitarianism of the nineteenth century gave way to the domination of the Unitarian Universalism movement in the twentieth century. Essentially, the Unitarian Universalists preach a faith in a one-world, one-religion typology. In its latest iteration, out of a desperate attempt to be seen as open, diverse and as tolerant as possible, the group accepts beliefs from just about every religious tradition in the world, ranging from Judaism to Buddhism. Unitarian Universalists teach that there is no one truth and that God speaks through all religions. Their warrant for such belief stems from heretical premises, such as that

Scripture exaggerates Jesus' miracles, that non-canonical "gospels" (for example, the "Gospel of Judas") are acceptable in that they tell us something about the life of Jesus, that Jesus was not born of the Virgin, and that doctrine is unnecessary in forming the basis of faith (to name just a few).

Aside from the obvious Arian heresy committed by denying the divinity of Christ, one point worth noting about Unitarians is their position on interreligious dialogue. Unitarians themselves don't want to make specific statements about faith, and, of course, this is what allows nominal Christians to join them and avoid living the Gospel message and the doctrines of Tradition fully. In essence, then, Unitarianism is the religious equivalent of practical atheism or political agnosticism. The Unitarian umbrella has now become an excuse for avoiding religious stands in the public square by shrouding itself in the language of pluralism, tolerance and diversity.

- ### Interreligious Dialogue Can Lead to a Denial that Jesus is God

Sadly, this modern desire for oneness and sameness in the name of a false peace has sparked an Arian revolution among Christians engaged in interreligious dialogue. There has been a strong push, particularly since the September 11 terrorist attacks on the United States, to redefine the Western understanding of Islam and to make sure that grass roots interreligious dialogue avoids the entanglement of clearly stating what makes the Christian different than the Jew or the Muslim—first and foremost, the belief that Jesus is God.

Arian tendencies have therefore crept into the Catholic Church by way of priests, brothers, nuns, and theologians who, desperate in their desire for any and all kinds of dialogue, have decided that it would be simply rude to "impose" the divinity of Jesus on a theological discussion. Some theologians have tried to use the dictates of the Second Vatican Council as an excuse to dismiss or marginalize the dogmas of the Faith in the name of engagement with the world. Especially in public forums, like centers of cultural or religious study in universities, local prayer services and interreligious exchanges, the political correctness that has crept into these European and American schools of thought has made it increasingly difficult to catechize the young and old alike. Although it is perfectly reasonable, even laudable, to want to dialogue with people of differing faiths, striving for greater peace through greater understanding as a means to serve humanity, it is not permissible to attempt to buy that peace by denying what makes a Christian a Christian: that Jesus is God.

CHAPTER FOUR

Pelagianism
Putting Man at the Center of the Universe

G OD NEVER INTENDED FOR US to work out our salvation alone. Out of His pure love He created us, and in His pure wisdom He knew we would need Him to guide us back to Him. Acting as the good shepherd, God sent His only-begotten Son into the world so that by hearing His voice and seeing His face, His flock might know Him personally and follow Him.

Pelagius was a layman in the earliest centuries of the Church who was so enthralled by the teachings of the Stoic philosophers that he began to believe that man was capable of his own salvation. He believed that, through virtue, man was capable of ascending to God, that the sheep could return without the Shepherd's help. For him, Jesus was a good example of how to live, but not an essential link to our eternal life.

Modern examples of Pelagianism are easy to spot in the rampant, narcissistic individualism that has gripped American society in the last fifty years. The spirit of Pelagius has also found its way into the Church in the form of psychotherapeutic spiritualities that allow a person to put himself at the center of his prayer life— in direct contradiction to the spiritual masters who have taught that God comes first.

- ## GOD PROTECTED HIS CHOSEN PEOPLE IN THE OLD TESTAMENT

God showed the Prophets that He was looking out for all of His people, first by testing them and then by revealing Himself. His reason for doing this was to make sure that we would remain faithful to Him by keeping Him at the center of our lives.

> And Jacob was left alone; and a man wrestled with him until the breaking of the day. When the man saw that he did not prevail against Jacob, he touched the hollow of his thigh; and Jacob's thigh was put out of joint as he wrestled with him. Then he said, "Let me go, for the day is breaking." But Jacob said, "I will not let you go, unless you bless me." And he said to him, "What is your name?" And he said, "Jacob." Then He said, "Your name shall no more be called Jacob, but Israel, for you have striven with God and with men, and have prevailed."[1]

God treats us as a true Father: giving us our inheritance as pure love-gift, but teaching us to work hard for what we have been given. In this way, He has looked after us as His people. He taught us that He would be both loving and faithful in His Word toward us. In so doing, He taught us to be faithful to Him. "[B]ut it is because the Lord loves you, and is keeping the oath which he swore to your fathers, that the Lord has brought you out with a mighty hand, and redeemed you from the house of bondage, from the hand of Pharaoh king of Egypt."[2] God taught us how to recognize Him within the people in our midst, showing us how to care for each other. He taught us to remain steadfast in our belief and warned us of what would happen when those who did not believe discovered that Jesus spoke of being one with the Father. He also

---

1. *Gen.* 32:24-28.
2. *Deut.* 7:8.

warned that if the unbelievers would crucify His Son, we would need to be prepared for a similar fate. He called each of us to be strong and to defend the faith in the Trinity, standing up to those who choose not to follow the path of the Good Shepherd.

My son, if sinners entice you, do not consent. If they say, "Come with us, let us lie in wait for blood, let us wantonly ambush the innocent; like Sheol let us swallow them alive and whole, like those who go down to the Pit; we shall find all precious goods, we shall fill our houses with spoil; throw in your lot among us, we will all have one purse—my son, do not walk in the way with them, hold back your foot from their paths; for their feet run to evil, and they make haste to shed blood."[3]

The Jesus and Judas imagery in the above passage from *Proverbs* is quite striking. Solomon foreshadows for us that Judas and the unbelievers would persecute Jesus and that He would be buried on our behalf. He explains how the betrayer would be more concerned about the common purse, about material goods, and would take for himself what was not his. In effect, Solomon tells us here that the deceiver will try to tempt the sheep so they would go astray from their Master who was more than willing to leave the ninety-nine to go after the one.

- JESUS IS REVEALED IN THE NEW TESTAMENT AS
  THE SAVIOR

I am the good shepherd. The good shepherd lays down His life for the sheep. He who is a hireling and not a shepherd, whose own, the sheep are not, sees the wolf coming and leaves the sheep and flees;

---

3. *Prov.* 1:10-16.

and the wolf snatches them and scatters them. He flees because he is a hireling and cares nothing for the sheep. I am the good shepherd; I know my own and my own know me, as the Father knows me and I know the Father; and I lay down my life for the sheep. And I have other sheep, that are not of this fold; I must bring them also, and they will heed my voice. So there shall be one flock, one shepherd. For this reason the Father loves me, because I lay down my life, that I may take it again. No one takes it from me, but I lay it down of my own accord. I have power to lay it down, and I have power to take it again; this charge I have received from my Father.[4]

No leader, business or government will ever look after the members of the flock like Jesus Christ does for us. Men and man-made institutions are simply hirelings, whereas He is the One who will stand up to the wolves. He knows us and we must know Him; He seeks the others who do not right now hear His voice. He is the shepherd who will lay down His life for all of us sheep, and He will do it of His own accord. Note well: no one else will take it from Him, but He will lay it down for all of us. In doing so, He will fulfill what the Father has asked of Him—and all of what we ask of Him.

Therefore are they before the throne of God, and serve Him day and night within His temple; and He who sits upon the throne will shelter them with His presence. They shall hunger no more, neither thirst any more; the sun shall not strike them, nor any scorching heat. For the Lamb in the midst of the throne will be their shepherd, and He will guide them to springs of living water; and God will wipe away every tear from their eyes.[5]

---

4. *John* 10:11-18.
5. *Rev.* 7:15-17.

Not only will He take care of our every need now, but also in the time to come. The Good Shepherd has always looked out for His people, and we must know how joyfully we depend on Him. Through and in Him, we know that whatever happens to us in this present life is in accord with the will of Christ. More than that, we know what will happen next, and that is to spend eternity with Him or to be cast away from Him.

[A]nd I heard a great voice from the throne saying, "Behold, the dwelling of God is with men. He will dwell with them, and they shall be His people, and God Himself will be with them; He will wipe away every tear from their eyes, and death shall be no more, neither shall there be mourning nor crying nor pain any more, for the former things have passed away."[6]

Despite all of the promises God has made throughout history—to love us, to be near us and to help us always—man continually chooses to rely on himself. He thinks of himself as being so advanced, so intelligent and so autonomous that he believes it is possible not only to control his immediate world but what will become of him in the next. The Judas Syndrome ensures that such thinking persists from age to age. But its archetypical example was Pelagius, who in the latter 4th century proposed that man was capable of achieving virtue (and ultimately his salvation) under his own power without the grace of God.

• Pelagius Denied the Need for Christ

Pelagius, born in Britain in 354, was well-educated and seemed initially to have had a good reputation, but he became too heavily

---

6. *Rev.* 21:3-4.

influenced by the pagan elements of Roman and Greek philosophies. The Stoics, for example, believed that man was capable of an ideal life through discipline and the study of philosophy, physics, logic and ethics. Accordingly, Pelagius regarded the human will as sufficient to attain all of the virtues, *including the theological virtues of faith, hope and love*, through intense training and strict discipline. This belief led him first to deny original sin and its effect on the human person, then to deny that concupiscence was a bad thing. Next, he denied the resurrection of the body, and finally, he denied that Jesus' life, death and resurrection were the key to our salvation. The followers of Pelagius, especially Caelestius, embraced these teachings and expanded upon them. They rejected the unique nature of the Gospel message, asserting that the laws provided by Moses in the Old Testament were as good a means to salvation as the teachings of Jesus.

- STS. JEROME AND AUGUSTINE WROTE OF OUR
  DEPENDENCE ON JESUS

Among the many early Church theologians who wrote against this apostasy, it is worth noting that St. Jerome—who lived from 347 to 420 and is perhaps best known for translating the Bible into Latin—engaged the Pelagians in the early 400s. As part of a dialogue about the extent to which man has free will and the extent to which man participates in his own salvation, Jerome was adamant that man was limited in what he could achieve without the help of grace. St. Augustine, bishop of Hippo in North Africa who lived from 354 to 430, became concerned for the people in his diocese because they had become confused by Pelagius's ideas of sin, grace and salvation. They had fallen prey to the Pelagian argument for the superiority of man's will over and against man's radical need for grace. In two important works, *Against Two Let-*

ters of the Pelagians and *On the Merits and Remission of Sins and On the Baptism of Infants*,[7] Augustine reaffirmed the theological arguments about sin, the need for Baptism and our need of grace.

> As therefore our first parents, by their subsequent return to righteous living, by which they are supposed to have been released from the worst penalty of their sentence through the blood of the Lord, were still not deemed worthy to be recalled to Paradise during their life on earth, so in like manner our sinful flesh, even if a man lead a righteous life in it after the remission of his sins, does not deserve to be immediately exempted from that death which it has derived from its propagation of sin.[8]

Augustine's point is that righteous living alone does not save us from death, meaning that we still need the grace and mercy of God in order to unite with God. In addition to affirming the importance of grace in salvation, Augustine explained that the good works we perform are somehow always tied to the God who created us. Even in the virtues that man can achieve with his own natural powers (such as the cardinal virtues of prudence, justice, temperance and fortitude), the Divine is always reaching out toward us in love and wisdom to assist us in our desire to reach Him.

> But who of us will say that by the sin of the first man free will perished from the human race? Through sin freedom indeed perished, but it was that freedom which was in Paradise, to have a full righteousness with immortality; and it is on this account that human

---

7. John A. Mourant and William J. Collinge, *trans. St. Augustine: Four Anti-Pelagian Writings*, vol. 86 of *The Fathers of the Church* (Washington, D.C.: The Catholic University of America Press, 1992).

8. On the Merits and Remission of Sins, and on the Baptism of Infants, Book 2:34:55. Philip Schaff, D.D., L.L.D., and Henry Wace, D.D., eds, *Augustine*, vol. V of *A Select Library of the Nicene and Post-Nicene Fathers of the Christian Church Second Series* (Grand Rapids, Michigan: WM B Eerdmans Publishing, 1904), p. 66.

nature needs divine grace, since the Lord says, "If the Son shall make you free, then shall ye be free indeed"—free of course to live well and righteously.[9]

In addition to the debate over original sin and the role of grace, Augustine argued with the Pelagians over the question of man's free will. The Pelagians argued that if God's plan for salvation in the redemptive work of Jesus Christ and the restorative work of the Holy Spirit were true, then it would follow that man is not ultimately free because God is somehow interceding all along the way. Augustine's reply to that was simple: *to choose to sin is not real freedom.* In fact, since man is sinful and more often than not chooses what is wrong, a life lived without some sort of saving mechanism, limited only to what man can achieve, is the truly limited life. To choose to follow God is ultimate freedom, because man is freed from the bondage of sin, from the bondage of making decisions for selfish or sinful reasons, and from the bondage of a nihilism that stems from a belief that life is limited to this physical world.

> [W]hat kind of liberty, I ask, can the bond-slave possess, except when it pleases him to sin? For he is freely in bondage who does with pleasure the will of his master. Accordingly, he who is the servant of sin is free to sin. And hence he will not be free to do right, until, being freed from sin, he shall begin to be the servant of righteousness. And this is true liberty, for he has pleasure in the righteous deed; and it is at the same time a holy bondage, for he is obedient to the will of God.[10]

---

9. A Treatise Against Two Letters of the Pelagians, Book 1, Chapter 5. Philip Schaff, D.D., L.L.D., *ed, Augustine,* vol. V of *A Select Library of the Nicene and Post-Nicene Fathers of the Christian Church* (New York: The Christian Literature Company, 1887), p. 378.

10. "The Enchiridion on Faith, Hope and Love," http://www.newadvent.org/fathers/1302.htm, July 4, 2006. Excerpted from *Nicene and Post-Nicene Fathers, Series One, Volume 3,* Chapter 30, Philip Schaff, D.D., LL.D., *ed.* (online edition, K. Knight, 2004).

A final point to be made about Augustine here is that when man gives himself over to sin, he becomes incapable of making judgments for the good. The more he strays from the will of God, the more he is incapable of seeking it. Furthermore, the more incapable he is of seeking God's will, the more he tends to seek his own. Without the freedom that comes from giving a life over to the living God, man is forever held as a slave to his passions.

The growing theological debate between Augustine and Pelagius prompted a series of diocesan hearings and synods. Bishop John of Jerusalem convoked a diocesan council in 415 to investigate the charge of heresy against his friend Pelagius. The proceedings were hampered, especially by Latin and Greek translation problems, so participants agreed to appeal to Rome for a decision. Before that happened, however, Gallic bishops began to investigate the charge of heresy and brought the matter to Bishop Eulogius of Caesarea, who also invoked a synod in 415. Again, problems came about with those proceedings, but Deacon Anianus of Celeda was able to argue against Pelagius, who answered by dismissing the charges as only the ravings of his follower Caelestius. (Two synods at Carthage and Mileve in North Africa agreed with Pelagius on this point.) By 417, Pope Innocent I had agreed with the definitions on original sin and the role of grace, and excluded Pelagius and Caelestius from communion. Both men submitted letters to Rome to justify their positions, but the Pope died before he could consider their pleas.

In the years that followed, Pelagius published a work on grace that leaned toward Augustine's definition, meaning he assented, first, to the possibility of a divine revelation about and through Jesus Christ, and secondly, to the existence of a kind of grace that aided men in choosing the good. Pelagius still taught, however, that the grace he was referring to related to the enlightenment or healing that can come from thinking good thoughts, reading the Bible, hearing good homilies, and so on. He even proposed that Baptism might be a good idea, not because there is some transformative mystery that occurs, but only to capture some positive effect from the ritual, or to protect against the possibility that there really is a Heaven.

Once Pope Zosimus took over in Rome for Innocent, the bishops of North Africa requested that he maintain the condemnation of Pelagius until he confessed that grace was necessary in every thought, word and deed of mankind. In 418, at the Council of Carthage, 200 bishops declared Pelagianism a heresy and wrote eight canons that closely followed Augustine,[11] affirming: the theology that death is a consequence of sin; the requirement that babies should be baptized because they are born under original sin; the theology that God's grace justifies the human race, relieving it of its past sins and assisting us in avoiding future sins; that Jesus Christ reveals God and His commandments to us and gives us the strength to abide by those commandments; the theology that good works are impossible without God's grace; that we must confess ourselves to be sinners; and even the saints must pray for the forgiveness of their trespasses, but in doing so they are also praying for us.

These canons are the structured, legal form of explaining how it is that we are radically dependent on God for the good we do and how much bad we do against Him and ourselves. The kind of humility they express is incompatible with the Judas Syndrome: when mankind comes to believe in its own ability more than in what he is capable of doing with God's help.

---

11. Henricus Denzinger, *Enchiridion Symbolorum*, 10th ed. (Rome: Herder & Co., 1908), 101-108.

• AGNOSTIC-INDIVIDUALISM IN AMERICA AS MODERN PELAGIANISM

Perhaps the clearest example of how Pelagianism has manifested itself in the modern world is in the rampant and ever-growing agnostic-individualism that infects wide swaths of cultural activity in the Western world: egalitarian-based modes of behavior in the workplace, a political tendency to ignore the religious foundations of moral and economic issues (largely under the misunderstood and misapplied dictum of separating church and state), and the anti-religious, anti-Church attitudes found in academia and the media. The foundations for such attitudes can be traced to a broader period in Western history that includes the Renaissance through the Enlightenment.

The Renaissance was a series of literary and cultural movements in the fourteenth, fifteenth and sixteenth centuries that began in Italy and eventually expanded into other parts of Europe. Participants, influenced by the growing humanism of the period, were initially interested in studying the ancient Greek and Roman empires for the purpose of proving how the cultural accomplishments of "modern" man rivaled those of antiquity. More than that, these Renaissance humanists believed it was possible to improve human society through a classical education that relied on ancient texts in a range of disciplines, including poetry, history, rhetoric and moral philosophy.

One abstract example of how this mentality changed the Western worldview is that prior to this period, when a work had been completed—whether it was academic, literary, poetic or artistic—the piece was dedicated in some way to God. Under the new intellectual paradigm, however, such works celebrated only that which is observable, including the person who created them. Beauty, therefore, and its practical application in art, was seen to be found only in the human form and deriving from the human mind. Goodness became a function of individual taste (over and against divine and ecclesiastical law), and truth was restricted to science; all things in and outside of nature were judged according only to the scientific method. Through these developments, God and the Church were not merely ignored but subjugated.

A second and more concrete example of the influence of Renaissance thinking on the life of Western Europe was the influence it had on the Protestant Reformers. Because Luther and Calvin had such strong tendencies toward predestination and the absolute rule of grace (over free will), it is quite possible that these "reformers" released the average believer from worrying about or working out their salvation. To the adherents of the new Protestant religions, there would have been very little reason to focus on the Christian life, since God was either going to extend grace to a person or He was not; by extension, He was either going to save a particular person or He was not. Practically speaking, that new mentality would have eliminated, for example, the need for the Sacraments.

Political developments in this time period and later ones impacted the worldview of the average citizen as well. The French Revolution, for example, was supposed to have started as a nonviolent expression of reform against King Louis XVI, who in response to earlier demands had created a National Assembly. In short order, that National Assembly tried to force reform of the Church in France, a reform that included, among other things, an oath of allegiance to the newly formed nation. As a result, nationalism began to grow at the expense of devotion to God and Church. Priests were forced to take loyalty oaths to the constantly changing national leadership, churches were forced to relinquish property, and the government assumed control over the practice of the Faith.

The impact of these changes extended to the academic world, including the way in which philosophy and theology were conceived and taught. The "Age of Enlightenment" refers to the thought of philosophers and writers of the eighteenth century, before the French Revolution, who put their faith into reason, science, culture and human thought. Set on their path by the likes of Descartes, Spinoza, Hobbes and Locke, these thinkers were cultural relativists who came to assume that progress in knowledge, technical achievement and moral values would come through observation of nature rather than through the study of authoritative sources such as the Bible. By extension, rationalism (as it is known) introduced a critical pattern of thought, which insisted that traditional beliefs should be examined only through reason and never faith.

The religious expression of rationalism came in the form of *Deism*.[12] Essentially, this is a philosophical paradigm that, while acknowledging a deity, rejected the details of Christian theology, including revelation, Sacraments, original sin, evil, miracles and the need for dogmatic teachings. Deists sought broad agreement on the major tenets of religion, but did not see religious unity as a necessity in the social order (so the Church became seen as a negative force). Deists believed that human experience should not be centered on the next life, but on the means of improving this one because worldly happiness was more important than religious salvation. From this paradigm was born not only modern utopian ideologies (such as Marxism) but also some of the most important philosophical and political foundations of American society. It has been well-documented that Thomas Jefferson, Benjamin Franklin, John Adams, James Madison, Thomas Paine and other notable founding fathers were Deists. This is important because it is through these men that the corresponding cultural and political traditions in America developed.

---

12. Notice the influences on modern Unitarianism.

Some Americans have seen the purpose and goal of the nation as the effort to realize the ancient biblical hope of a just and compassionate society. Others have struggled to shape the spirit of their lives and the laws of the nation in accord with the ideals of republican citizenship and participation. Yet others have promoted dreams of manifest destiny and national glory.[13]

To put this another way: from its beginnings American culture can be divided along three major lines[14]: the biblical tradition, the

---

13. Robert N. Bellah, Richard Madsen, William M. Sullivan, Ann Swidler and Steven M. Tipton. *Habits of the Heart: Individualism and Commitment in American Life* (Berkeley, California: University of California Press, Updated Edition 1996), p. 27.

14. The biblical language of the American tradition can best be understood by studying John Winthrop, who lived from 1588 to 1649, was well-educated, came from a good family, and was known to have maintained a deep Puritan religious conviction. He was the first governor of Massachusetts Bay Colony and is famous for a 1630 sermon titled, *A Model of Christian Charity*, in which he describes a "city set upon a hill." For him and others in the biblical tradition, success does not mean material wealth but the creation of a genuinely ethical and spiritual community. The republican language of American tradition can best be understood by looking at the life of Thomas Jefferson, who lived from 1743 to 1826, was well-educated, from the agrarian class of Virginia, and was the author of the Declaration of Independence. To him, while all people are not exactly equal in every respect, what makes people equal is both the variety of what they can offer society and also that they choose to enter the public square and offer what they have. What this means is that the republican ideal is the independent worker, farmer or businessman who is self-sufficient and participates in the political life of the country.

Utilitarian individualism, which developed from the Calvinist tradition, focuses on moral discipline and a type of self-help preoccupied with earthly rewards. The best way to understand utilitarian individualism is to look at Benjamin Franklin, who lived from 1706 to 1790, and is viewed in history as the quintessential American, the archetypal poor boy who became successful and important. Franklin gave expression to what many feel is the most important thing about America: the chance to get ahead.

Expressive individualism has little to do with material acquisition; it is a life rich in experience, luxuriating in the sensual as well as the intellectual. Above all, it is a life focused on one's depth of feeling and the expression of those feelings. The best way to understand this kind of individualism is to view Walt Whitman, who lived from 1819 to 1892, was the son of an artisan, self-educated and self-made as a printer, journalist and poet. The reason he is considered to be the best example of this kind of individualism is republican tradition and the individualist tradition, which can further be subdivided into utilitarian individualism and expressive individualism.

Although individualism in America was originally about an aspiration to be self-reliant, independent and free from external control, it became a madness driven by the utilitarian focus on material goods and the expressive obsession with the self. Each of the three American traditions views the human person as a self-made creation focused only on his own authority. Because of the Judas Syndrome, Pelagianism today is found in the increasingly human-centered focus of society.

Witness, for one example, the unhealthy obsession Americans have with psychological analysis, driving a multi-billion dollar industry in self-help, life-coaching and motivational products. Making matters worse is modern communications—including the radio, television, print media and the internet—which have so dramatically increased the sources of specialty information that no one person is compelled to go beyond his infantile opinions or pleasures or to grasp the world in a wider context. The most serious side effect of such a fundamental shift in human culture is that more and more Americans distrust authority and tradition, including God and the Church.

- Pelagianism in Modernist Spirituality and Homiletics

Sadly, these attitudes have crept into the Church as well. Since the Second Vatican Council, too much of spiritual formation and direction has been based on a psychotherapeutic worldview. Priests

---

because his poetry was all about what was going on inside of him. It had little to do with the world except for how he viewed the world and how it affected him.

For more information see Ibid.

and religious turned blindly to the day's developments in psychology and applied them to the spiritual life. But although the spiritual life is related to the psychological, relational and intellectual development of the person, it is not the same thing. The practical result, particularly within seminaries, convents and monasteries, was that those in religious vocations were being trained to become miniature therapists, more interested in their own feelings and the feelings of their retreatants and parishioners than in the deepening of their experience with the wisdom and love of God.

Spiritual maturation involves, at first, an instinctive acceptance of rules and laws provided to us by parents, elders, priests and bishops. Later, it evolves into an intellectual pursuit aimed at building a greater understanding of theology and the deepening of a related spirituality. Finally, spiritual maturation enters into a phase that removes selfishness and opens us up to an exploration of God on His terms. Fixating instead on a "spirituality of emotions," on spirituality-as-therapy, has diminished the Church's ability to help the modern believer ascend to greater heights of awareness of God, as well as the ultimate reduction of the self in relation to Him.

Another area where one might find Pelagianism in the modern Church is in homilies, in variations on harmless-sounding but heretical sayings such as, "God helps those who help themselves." Priests encourage their flock to "get right with God" by "picking themselves up by their own bootstraps" or through better time management or organizational skills. There's also a Pelagian undertone to the clergy's desire to modernize or "meet people where they are." As an example, the advent of the Life Teen Mass has done much to reaffirm for teenagers that they don't have to conform to the Tradition, that they don't have to attend liturgy with their family, and that their social grouping should be given special treatment. There is nothing wrong with creating events that specifically appeal to teenagers so they can learn in their own style and at their own pace, of course, but to alter the liturgy in order to cater to the infantile desires of the spoiled few is not only an affront to the Tradition itself but to the God who gave it to us. (This experience can be found in the development of children's liturgies after Vatican II and also the experimental modes of catechesis developed in the 1970s and 1980s.)

These examples show the tendency to focus on man instead of on God (which is exactly what Pelagius did . . . and Judas too for that matter), ultimately encouraging the person receiving information to place Himself before God and the Church.

God came to us as the Good Shepherd in order to assist us on our journey back to Him. We rely on Him and His grace in both the good that we do and in the bad from which we need to recover. There is no confusion about this. Pelagius convinced himself and tried to convince others that man did not need God, that humans were capable of all that was needed to achieve a life well-lived and to attain salvation. We know this is not possible, and we are thankful because He is the Good Shepherd. He knows us, and when we allow ourselves, we will know Him. But only because He first makes his voice heard.

CHAPTER FIVE

Iconoclasm
Destroying the Face of Christ

B Y HIS LOVE, GOD CREATED MAN in His image, and through His wisdom He revealed Himself in the flesh. His Son established the Church, and His Spirit sanctifies it. For this we offer our entire selves—body, soul and spirit—to praise, honor and worship Him by acknowledging our experience of Him, by striving to learn more about Him, by loving Him and by serving Him from now until the end of time. The normal, ordinary process for this interaction with God begins and ends with the prayers of the Church (which is liturgy) and with our own personal prayers (which in some way are always derived from the prayers of the community).

Even from before the time of Christ, the common and expected means of liturgy and personal prayer have included—and should include—all of our physical senses: sight, smell, sound, taste and touch. Knowing full well that no image of the divine nature of God could ever be created (especially since this is so far beyond the comprehension of man), we can deepen our relationship with God through the image of God in Jesus, the image of God in us, and the images He asked us to create by our own hands: icons, statues, and other forms of sacred art.

The iconoclasts of the seventh and eighth centuries had much different ideas. Leo III, a Byzantine emperor, and a host of supposedly religious men decided that Christians shouldn't be allowed to write, paint, sculpt, or in any way depict God in art. These men believed that doing so was a sin against the second commandment (which forbids the worship of graven images). Through the Judas Syndrome, iconoclasm is alive and well today, found among politicians who shed their moral and religious consciences at the door of legislative chambers, municipalities that ban Christian displays at Christmas, and parishes that build churches that don't look like churches.

• THE IMAGE OF GOD IN THE OLD TESTAMENT

"Then God said, 'Let Us make man in our image, after our likeness'. . . So God created man in His own image, in the image of God He created him; male and female He created them."[1]

God is not only imprinted in the world in the spiritual realm (for example, the way God is imprinted within the soul of a man) but also by fiat in the material realm. God commanded His people to build temples in His honor, with altars worthy of His name. In so doing, God helped our forefathers in faith to understand the difference between building an edifice to honor the one, true God and the ancient pagan practices of constructing buildings for conjuring false gods and fashioning talismans to perform magical spells. God also asked mankind to create these places of worship with specific directions for constructing them, in order to aid us in knowing how to make our worship holy.

You shall not make gods of silver to be with me, nor shall you make for yourselves gods of gold. An altar of earth you shall make for me and sacrifice on it your burnt offerings, your sheep and your oxen; in

---

1. *Gen.* 1:26-27.

every place where I cause my name to be remembered I will come to you and bless you.[2]

God was so personally involved with aiding us in our worship that He also instructed us to build Him a sanctuary and explained how to make the tabernacle. "And let them make me a sanctuary, that I may dwell in their midst. According to all that I show you concerning the pattern of the tabernacle, and of all its furniture, so you shall make it."[3] Following this verse in *Exodus* is the specific instruction for building the Ark, and in a later chapter is the blueprint for designing the angels to adorn His vessel for the Covenant. Bez'alel also made the table for the bread of presence and "the vessels of pure gold which were to be upon the table, its plates and dishes for incense, and its bowls and flagons with which to pour libations."[4]

Later, when Solomon was able to build the Temple of the Lord, he did so not merely to meet God's specifications, but also to reproduce the heavenly kingdom on earth.

In the inner sanctuary he made two cherubim of olivewood, each ten cubits high. Five cubits was the length of one wing of the cherub, and five cubits the length of the other wing of the cherub; it was ten cubits from the tip of one wing to the tip of the other.... both cherubim had the same measure and the same form.[5]

This structure was meant both to glorify God and to raise up mankind. To serve in the Temple and for the people of God, He also called forth certain men from among His chosen people to become priests, who would lead His people in worship. These men

---

2. *Ex.* 20:23-24.
3. *Ex.* 25:8-9.
4. *Ex.* 37:16.
5. *1 Kgs.* 6:23-25.

were specifically dedicated as a means of ensuring that we could preserve truth, goodness and beauty in worship.

> And the Lord said to Moses, "Bring the tribe of Levi near, and set them before Aaron the priest, that they may minster to him. They shall perform duties for him and for the whole congregation before the tent of the meeting, as they minister at the tabernacle; they shall have charge of all the furnishings of the tent of meeting, and attend to the duties for the people of Israel as they minister at the tabernacle. And you shall give the Levites to Aaron and his sons; they are wholly given to him from among the people of Israel."[6]

- ## The Image of God in the New Testament

Later, creation rejoiced as God became man, and the images that God had instructed to be built were given the context that had awaited mankind from the beginning of time. Through the coming of Jesus, we were given not merely images to aid us in worship, we were given the true image of the invisible God.

> He is the image of the invisible God, the first-born of all creation; for in Him all things were created, in heaven and on earth, visible and invisible, whether thrones or dominions or principalities or authorities—all things were created through Him and for Him. He is before all things, and in Him all things hold together. He is the head of the body, the church; He is the beginning, the first-born from the dead, that in everything He might be pre-eminent.[7]

Material goods, when properly designed by well-formed believ-

---

6. *Num.* 3:5-9.
7. *Col.* 1:15-18.

ers, can become vehicles through which we are brought up into the power of God.

> And a woman who had had a flow of blood for twelve years and had spent all her living upon physicians and could not be healed by any one, came up behind Him, and touched the fringe of His garment; and immediately her flow of blood ceased. And Jesus said, "Who was it that touched me? [. . .] Some one touched me; for I perceive that power has gone forth from me."[8]

Just as the hem of Jesus' garment could transmit something of Him, so too can icons, statues, paintings and other material. The woman in the story was not confused that Jesus' garment *was* Jesus; instead, she knew in faith that if she approached Him merely to touch His garment—in the mode of humble supplication—Jesus would be merciful and heal her. An important point to note is the material—because it was either created by God directly or God created the artisan who created it in honor of Him—for human creations are to be used for the glory of God.

Just as the temple, the sanctuary and the tabernacle were built for the Jews in the time prior to the coming of Christ, Jesus reaffirms the need to build churches for the gathering of the community of believers, to erect altars to consecrate the bread and wine into His Body and Blood, and to ordain priests for the care of the souls left in the charge of the Church under the guidance of His Holy Spirit. In His command to do these things in memory of Him, we were told how to conduct the liturgy (our primary communal prayer) and how to conduct ourselves in the liturgy. This command is also part of the revelation that liturgy is what we will "do" in Heaven. In other words, what we do here is an

---

8. *Luke* 8:43-46.

image of what is occurring in Heaven. Church and the liturgy are important because it is there that we find our primary look at and participation in Heaven.

> At once I was in the Spirit, and lo, a throne stood in heaven, with one seated on the throne! And He who sat there appeared like jasper and carnelian, and round the throne was a rainbow that looked like an emerald. Round the throne were twenty-four thrones, and seated on the thrones were twenty-four elders, clad in white garments, with golden crowns upon their heads. From the throne issue flashes of lighting, and voices and peals of thunder, and before the throne burn seven torches of fire, which are the seven spirits of God; and before the throne there is as it were a sea of glass, like crystal. And round the throne, on each side of the throne, are four living creatures, full of eyes in front and behind: the first living creature like a lion, the second living creature like an ox, the third living creature with the face of a man, and the fourth living creature like a flying eagle. And the four living creatures, each of them with six wings, are full of eyes all round and within, and day and night they never cease to sing, "Holy, holy, holy is the Lord God Almighty; who was and is and is to come!" And whenever the living creatures give glory and honor and thanks to Him who is seated on the throne, who lives for ever and ever, the twenty-four elders fall down before Him who is seated on the throne and worship Him who lives for ever and ever; they cast their crowns before the throne, singing, "Worthy art thou, our Lord and God, to receive glory and honor and power, for thou didst create all things, and by thy will they existed and were created."[9]

9. *Rev.* 4:2-11.

We will see the face of Christ in Heaven, and we can gaze upon the face of Christ on earth.[10] Since God came into the world in order that man might become more like God, it is a perfectly logical reality that He would give us the tools we need to praise and worship Him: the tools for communal and personal prayer. God clearly intended for us not only to build sanctuaries for our worship, but also to create certain images that would facilitate the relationship we are called to have with Him. This was established in both the Old and the New Covenants because God knew mankind.

• Confusion Over the Second Commandment

God saw how ancient peoples had worshiped the idols of false gods, and that even those who were among His chosen people had relapsed and made new idols (for example, the golden calf). These were the precursors to Judas, who shunned the true, created image of God in Jesus Christ, betraying Him for the false idols of power and prestige. Still, there have been others, like the Muslims, who object to picturing God in any way, due largely to a misreading of the Second Commandment.

You shall not make for yourself an idol or a likeness of anything in heaven above, or in the earth beneath, or in the waters under the earth. You shall not bow down to them or serve them, for I, the Lord your God, am a jealous God, recompensing the sins of the fathers on the children to the third and fourth generation of those who hate Me; but showing mercy to thousands, to those who love Me and keep My commandments.[11]

---

10. We should gaze upon the faces of the evangelists, the Apostles, the martyrs, the Church Fathers and the saints as well. The four creatures mentioned above (lion, calf, man and eagle) are representations of the writers of the Gospel. All of these forefathers in the Faith provide examples of how we should live in this world.

11. *Ex.* 20:4-6.

This commandment is repeated in the fourth chapter of *Deuteronomy*, where the people of Israel were enjoined against making false images of gods. The context of the Deuteronomic passage is an important one because it speaks to the two parts of the issue raised by the Second Commandment in *Exodus*. First, man should never try to depict the inner life of God, and secondly, man should never put any false god before the one, true God. This second part is obvious: it is wrong to create and celebrate mythological beings. It is additionally wrong to exacerbate such a sin by lifting up material objects that bear a likeness to a false god, imagining them with a kind of magical power. In fact, this is the context in which idol worship is again mentioned in chapter fifteen of the Wisdom of *Solomon*. There it specifically mentions "human art" with "dead images" that create "a desire in fools."

It is the first issue raised by the Second Commandment that requires further explanation. Man is never to try to illustrate the fullness of God, His inner life, His essence, because the inner life of God is utterly incomprehensible in human terms. Because, however, God has revealed Himself to us in myriad forms throughout the Old Testament and in the very Son of God Himself—and also by asking us to build temples, altars and icons to reflect what has been shown to us—then not only are we not wrong for trying to depict the God who walked among us, but it becomes our *duty*. Sadly, those who would become iconoclasts had lost sight of this as early as the fourth century:

I came to a villa called Anablatha, and, as I was passing, saw a lamp burning there. Asking what place it was, and learning it to be a church, I went in to pray, and found there a curtain hanging on the doors of the said church, dyed and embroidered. It bore an image either of Christ or of one of the saints; I do not rightly remember whose the image was. Seeing this, and being loth that an image of a man should be hung up in Christ's church contrary to the teaching of the Scriptures, I tore it asunder and advised the custodians of the place to use it as a winding sheet for some poor person.[12]

This attitude grew over the next four hundred years, when the apex of iconoclasm resulted in the destruction of religious art in the Eastern Roman Empire during the eighth and ninth centuries.

• DESTRUCTION OF ICONS UNDER LEO III, BYZANTINE EMPEROR

Influenced by earlier heresies such as Gnosticism (which rejected matter and therefore all depictions of it) and Arianism (which rejected the divinity of Jesus and therefore any depiction of Him as God), and also because of the growing influence of the Muslim iconoclasm under Yezid I and Yezid II (caliphs in Damascus from 680 to 683 and 720 to 724, respectively), Leo III, Byzantine Emperor from 716 to 741, instigated the destruction of any representations of God and the persecution of anyone who used icons in prayer, especially monks. His policy was based on the heretical belief that the veneration of images created superstition among Christians, on the false argument that the use of images was a deterrent in the conversion of Muslims and Jews, on the arrogant assumption that the Church needed to be purified by him, and finally on the desire to extend his own influence in the Church by exhorting the Patriarch of Constantinople to exercise greater control over his bishops and priests.

More than all of these, however, Leo III and his followers

---

12. Epiphanius, Ep. 51, 9. Philip Schaff, D.D., L.L.D., and Henry Wace, D.D., *eds*, *A Select Library of the Nicene and Post-Nicene Fathers of the Christian Church* (Buffalo and New York, 1900; reprinted Grand Rapids, Michigan: WM B Eerdmans Publishing, 1952).

(such as Constantine of Nacolia and Thomas of Claudiopolis) were driven by a growing distaste for liturgy, piety, prayer and, ultimately, monastic spirituality. In 726, Leo III made it illegal to make images of God and required that existing images be destroyed. This practice grew so violent that relics were pulverized, the bodies of saints were dug up and burned, and monks were banished, tortured, or put to death. Meanwhile, Patriarch Germanus I in the East and Pope Gregory II in the West defended the ancient practice that allowed for the depiction of Christ, while Eastern monks stood strong in defending their monasteries' use of icons.

An additional consequence of Leo III's heresy was the exacerbation of tensions between the remnants of the Eastern Roman Empire and the Western Roman Empire. There were a series of political struggles that began when the western portion of the empire fell to barbarian tribes of northern Europe, leading to the eventual growth and influence of the Frankish kings. Eventually the popes, who had essentially become the political leaders of Western Europe from the fifth through the eighth centuries, refused to pay taxes and homage to the Byzantine Emperor, who was the heir to the Roman throne. By the time of the iconoclastic controversy, Gregory II had already refused to pay taxes under his papacy, and the people of Italy refused to comply with Leo's demand that icons be destroyed.[13]

Political tensions exploded when the iconodules (those who supported the use of icons in prayer) set up a rival emperor named Cosmas. Religious controversy came to a head when Leo tried to exercise control over and expand the territory of the Constantinopolitan Patriarchate by seizing religious property in Sicily and Southern Italy. An underlying tension already existed over the

---

13. Southern Italy and Sicily were still heavily influenced by the Byzantine Empire, and thus, the Greek language and the Byzantine form of the liturgy were used there.

growing relationship between the Pope and the Frankish kings who were trying to exert their own control over the Church in the West. As a consequence, Leo declared an even more severe edict in 730. That year, Rome convoked a local synod to condemn the destruction of icons and to level the canonical penalty of excommunication upon anyone who did.

Upon his death in 741, Leo's son Constantine V continued the persecution. In 754, Constantine demanded that a local council at Constantinople be called to make the veneration of icons illegal under Church law,[14] to elect a new patriarch who would enforce the emperor's decrees among the eastern bishops, to abolish monasticism, and to condemn Germanus, St. John of Damascus and monks from Cyprus, all of whom defended icons. Constantine's son, Leo IV, was more lenient toward the use of icons and allowed monks to return to their monasteries. In fact, his wife, the Empress Irene, was privately an iconodule and had many of the empire's icons hidden at the imperial palace so that they could be saved from destruction. Nicetas I, who replaced Patriarch Constantine II after his beheading, continued to support iconoclasm, most likely out of political expediency. When Leo IV died, his son was too young to ascend to the throne so the Empress Irene acted in his place.

Irene restored icons and other religious relics to churches, encouraged the religious practice of invoking saints as intercessors, and allowed for the free operation of monasteries. Patriarch Paul IV, who followed Nicetas I, resigned as a result of his former support of iconoclasm, and Tarasius was elected in his place. Together, Tarasius and Irene worked to convoke an ecumenical council to establish that the local synod of 754 was heretical and that icons

---

14. Up to that time, the laws against the veneration of images were limited to the civil realm.

should be defended. With the agreement of the bishops in the West under the direction of the Pope, the seventh ecumenical council was convened in Nicea in 787. The council declared that images may be venerated but not adored and that the reverence given to icons, statues and religious art is relative to what they represent. Anathemas were pronounced against the iconoclasts, and Patriarch Germanus, St. John of Damascus and George of Cyprus were praised for their efforts to resist the heresy. The canons of the council also demanded the restoration of monasteries. Unfortunately, by 813 the iconoclasts had regained power and began another severe round of persecution, which lasted until roughly 842.[15]

Iconoclasm in the West existed on a significantly smaller scale, but was found to exist in the dioceses of Turin and Bordeaux, as well as under some of the Frankish kings who, relying on a poor translation of the Council of Nicea, encouraged the destruction of images.

- Sts. John of Damascus and Theodore of Stoudios Defend Icons and the Faith

St. John of Damascus, who lived from roughly 676 to 749, was originally a chief administrator for the Muslim caliph in Syria, but eventually entered the St. Saba Monastery near Jerusalem. He became a monk, priest and writer renowned in both the Eastern and Western Churches. He is credited with writing a passionate defense of the ancient practice of venerating icons in his letters *Against those Who Destroy Sacred Images*. In those compositions, John establishes clearly that the Church has always maintained

---

15. The Feast of Orthodoxy, celebrated in the East on February 19, commemorates the return of icons to churches.

various practices for adoring God on the one hand and showing adoration for the Blessed Mother and the saints on the other.

We adore only the Creator and Maker of things, God, to whom we offer *latria* since God is to be adored according to His nature. We also adore the holy mother of God, not as God, but as mother of God according to the flesh. We also adore the saints, the chosen friends of God, by whom we have easy access to him.[16]

John also makes clear that the Church has neither condoned the attempt to make an image of the nature of God nor encouraged the lifting up of those created images as gods themselves.

We should certainly fall into error if we should make an image of the invisible God; since that which is not corporeal, nor visible, nor circumscribed, nor imagined, cannot be depicted at all. Again, we should act impiously if we thought images made by men were gods, and bestowed honors upon them as if they were. But we do not admit to doing any of these things.[17]

Another notable defender of the practice of praying with holy icons was St. Theodore of Stoudios, who lived from 759 to 826. A monk at the Stoudios monastery in Constantinople, he defended and energized monasticism and opposed the destruction of the holy images.

The Council of Nicea II derived a number of its canons from these two saints. In addition to the prohibition against the destruction of holy images, it is important to note three others. Canon seven not only returns honor to the veneration of relics, but requires that all churches contain them. That canon makes clear that no church can be consecrated without them. Canon nine requires that iconoclastic writings be considered heresy and

---

16. "Against Those Who Destroy Sacred Images," Or. 3, 41 in *The Teachings of the Church Fathers*, John R. Willis, S.J., *ed.* (Ignatius Press: San Francisco, 2002), p.5.

17. "Against Those Who Destroy Sacred Images," Or. 2, 5 in Ibid.

that future generations should avoid such a lapse in faith. Finally, Canon thirteen requires the return of ecclesiastical buildings to the monks or bishops from whom they were taken.

In the late medieval period, it is fair to say that the Protestants were among the first to renew the heresy. The radical Reformers' desire to excuse themselves from much of the ancient faith—including the particular design of churches, the use of legitimate altars, the writing of icons, the painting of pictures, the building of statues, the lighting of candles—is an example of just how much their hubris clouded their choices. Taking the corpus from the cross, building churches to look like Greek temples (or modern banks), destroying statues of the saints, and removing stained-glass windows had the additional effect of impacting catechesis in those churches. In an attempt to claim some moral, spiritual or theological high ground (in that the Reformers would ultimately trumpet their righteousness over and against Roman "idolatry" and the "magical" claim of turning bread into the Body of Christ), they inadvertently reduced Christianity to an essentially personal and emotional response to God, not the proper sacramental response articulated in both Scripture and Tradition. In disregarding the artistic representations of Christ, Mary, the Apostles, the martyrs and all the saints, the Reformers created an institutional solipsism from which they never recovered. The evidence for this is actually being played out among mainline Protestant denominations, which choose to govern themselves through polling data and a naive approach to ecclesiology that is attributable to their historic disdain toward the ancient practices of the Church of the East and West.

- Separation of the Icon of Faith from Public Policy

Modern secular iconoclasm has taken a decidedly antagonistic turn toward the Church in recent years, as legislators in the

United States, hiding behind the separation of church and state clause in the Constitution, have not only tried to marginalize politicians with sincerely held religious beliefs but also Christian citizens. The increasingly secular atmosphere in the American public square is making it increasingly difficult for the true believer to dedicate himself to a life with God. For example, witness the numerous lawsuits and lower-court decisions that have required courthouses to remove the Ten Commandments from their walls or in their lobbies. This is not only an affront to Judeo-Christian belief but also an affront to the legal system, which is rooted in divine and natural law.

Western Europe has followed suit in many of the same ways as the United States. It is no secret, or mere oversight, that the constitution of the European Union intentionally avoids any mention of the Christianity that underlies the continent's culture and traditions. In addition, when drafting the various requirements for admitting new countries to become members of the Union, again there were clauses that expressly restricted the implementation of laws in those countries that would be reflective of their historically Christian values—laws against abortion on demand, same-sex marriage, and so on.

• DESTRUCTION OF CHRISTIAN DISPLAYS

A second example of how modern America is denying God's image is in how municipalities are making it increasingly difficult to display Christian religious symbolism at Easter and Christmas. Even if one believes that the states should not be in the business of endorsing one religion or another—which is a reasonable position— one should not also expect the broader regulations that prohibit such exhibitions in public spaces. A third example of iconoclasm in America, which has a more dramatic impact, though it may not be so immediately obvious, is found in the ways the entertainment industry insults and degrades the ancient Christian faith. Young and old alike are bombarded by movies, television shows, music and advertising urging them to deny their maker, to disrespect their parents, to mock the Church and to give in to their most base and egotistical demands. This form of iconoclasm is one that shatters the image of God that exists *in our tradition.*

• CHURCHES THAT DON'T LOOK LIKE CHURCHES

Certainly there are external forces that try to get us to tear down our icons, our crosses, our statues, our paintings, and whatever other visible signs demonstrate that we are Christians of the ancient Church. The greatest threats to Christianity, however, often come from within its own ranks. Consider the historical examples. Not only were Christians heavily involved in the first persecution against depicting God artistically, but also it was radical Christian "reformers" who, in thinking it was also their job to purify the Church in the late Middle Ages, were involved in the second major persecution; of the way churches were built and how Jesus was to be visually depicted in them (no icons, no corpus on the cross, no tabernacle, no altars). These actions were a reflection of the hatred for Roman practice at the time. Sadly, in recent decades we have witnessed too many Catholic parishes that have gone the way of Protestant churches, stripping them bare of all that is sacred. This time the Church did not need an iconoclastic persecutor; we are doing it to ourselves.

Those who seek to build churches in a modern, "auditorium" style often cite economic motives.[18] They say that the traditional

---

18. This point is not intended against communities that are truly poor or oppressed and must do what they can in order to create a proper space. The reference is to fully-formed parishes that simply want to crowd more people into pews.

style of the Western Church (mainly cruciform in shape) is too narrow and can't hold enough people, or that church buildings must be "multipurpose" in design. When such arguments don't convince people, they resort to phony theological arguments, asserting that a round nave, for example, is like a circle without a beginning or an end, that it represents a whole, a unity among the people; or that the bare walls are there to assist the believer into internalizing the message of the Gospel (as opposed to being distracted by all those statues and stained glass); or that the altars and tabernacles should not be adorned because Jesus was a simple artisan, after all, a healer—a social worker of sorts. These minimalists pretend to want Church buildings and worship to focus on Jesus-as-humble-servant, hiding behind the claim that people have become too dependent on "externals" instead of "inviting Jesus into their hearts."

What those minimalists forget is that these kinds of churches contradict what God commanded us to do in the first place.

The Lord said to Moses, "On the first day of the first month you shall erect the tabernacle of the tent of meeting. And you shall put in it the ark of the testimony, and you shall screen the ark with the veil. And you shall bring in the table, and set its arrangements in order; and you shall bring in the lampstand, and set up its lamps. And you shall put the golden altar for incense before the ark of the testimony, and set up the screen for the door of the tabernacle. You shall set the altar of burnt offering before the door of the tabernacle of the tent of meeting, and place the laver between the tent of meeting and the altar, and put water in it. And you shall set up the court round bout, and hang up the screen for the gate of the court. Then you shall take the anointing oil, and anoint the tabernacle and all that is in it, and consecrate it and all its furniture; and it shall become holy. You shall also anoint the altar of burnt offering and all its utensils, and consecrate the altar and the altar shall be most holy . . . Then you shall bring

Aaron and his sons to the door of the tent of meeting, and shall wash them with water, and put upon Aaron the holy garments, and you shall anoint him and consecrate him, that he may serve me as priest. You shall bring his sons and put coats on them, as you anointed their father, that they may serve me as priests: and their anointing shall admit them to a perpetual priesthood throughout their generations" . . . So Moses finished the work. Then the cloud covered the tent of meeting, and the glory of the Lord filled the tabernacle . . . For throughout all their journeys the cloud of the Lord was upon the tabernacle by day, and fire was in it by night, in the sight of all the house of Israel.[19]

Moreover, in chapters 31 and 33 of *Exodus,* it is explained that Bezalel and Aholiab were given the gifts of the Holy Spirit in order to be able to build the tabernacle. So God not only gave directions about how to build churches and tabernacles, but also *endowed people with special gifts to do so.* It follows that churches should not be designed by committees looking for the most economical multi-use space they can get, but by those with a special charism who put the worship of God first.

Without denying that it is possible to become unduly fixated on the externals of worship, it must also be admitted that stripping down old churches and designing profane new ones has resulted in a further degradation of the proper respect and awe that is properly due our God. Churches were intended by God for us to know He is among us (not that we deny God is around us everywhere, but that there is a space reserved for our praise and worship of Him in a solemn and special way). Churches are *the* place for our sacred liturgy—meaning that they should look, feel, smell, sound and taste sacred—so that they lift us up to God, not drag God down to us. But the Judas Syndrome would deny us the vision of His face.

---

19. *Ex.* 40:1-15, 33-34, 38

CHAPTER SIX

Macedonianism
Minimizing the Holy Spirit

THE HOLY SPIRIT IS THE THIRD PERSON of the Trinity who has existed before all time and is consubstantial with the Father and the Son. He was with us in creation and He will be with us in all things through the end of days. He is the unique personhood of God, illuminating the path that points us to the Christ who redeemed us and to the Father who created us. The Holy Spirit is the Paraclete—the comforter and the advocate— our eternal advocate before the judgment seat of Christ. Filled with pure goodness and beauty, He does all of these things so that we may become more like the one, triune God and attain eternal unification with Him.

An early churchman named Macedonius was bitter about his removal from appointments in the city of Constantinople because it was found that he was sympathetic to the Arians. Even though he left his post, he remained in the city and began writing that the Holy Spirit was a mere created spiritual being to be counted equally among the many demons and angels.

Today we find Macedonianism in the New Age movement, which in recent years has also become associated with radical environmentalists. These groups tend to reduce the spirit of god to a presence not unlike the mythological "mother nature." Although it is laudable to want to protect God's creation, these groups tend to be pantheistic and draw their adherents away from the true teaching of the Faith. In the Church, this heresy can be found in reductionist spiritualities that more readily resemble twelve-step programs then they do a true devotion to the Third Person of the Trinity; in prayers and prayer services they embrace an extreme naturalism that exhibits the same reappearance of Macedonianism as do the environmentalists.

THE HOLY SPIRIT IN THE OLD TESTAMENT

The Holy Spirit spoke through the prophets and was recognized by the leaders of men. He inspired His chosen people and led them out of Egypt, helping them all along in their journey. "And the Lord went before them by day in a pillar of cloud to lead them along the way, and by night in a pillar of fire to give them light, that they might travel by day and by night; the pillar of cloud by day and the pillar of fire by night did not depart from before the people."[1] All along the way, He protected them against their enemies.

> At the blast of thy nostrils the waters piled up, the floods stood up in a heap; the deeps congealed in the heart of the sea. The enemy said, "I will pursue, I will overtake, I will divide the spoil, my desire shall have its fill of them." Thou didst blow with thy wind, the sea covered them; they sank as lead in the mighty waters.[2]

The Holy Spirit gave Himself freely so that we might understand, believe and become more like the God who created us. "The Lord said to Moses, 'See, I have called by name Bez'alel the Son of Uri, son of Hur, of the tribe of Judah: and I have filled him with the Spirit of God, with ability and intelligence, with knowledge

---

1. *Ex.* 13:21-22.
2. *Ex.* 15:8-10.

and craftsmanship."³ He was and is present in the material that God commanded us to use in His worship. It was the Holy Spirit who was present as Moses used the oils to ordain Aaron and to consecrate the tabernacle.⁴ Finally, it was Christ who built His Church upon the Holy Spirit; for as it was written, "Wisdom has built her house, she has set up her seven pillars."⁵

• THE HOLY SPIRIT IN THE NEW TESTAMENT

With the guidance of the Holy Spirit, it is the Church that draws believers into communion with God. He was sent to sanctify the new order that was established in Jesus and to make God's plan known to all. "But when the Counselor comes, whom I shall send to you from the Father, even the Spirit of truth, who proceeds from the Father, He will bear witness to me."⁶ Because nothing can be achieved by human power alone, the Holy Spirit will be the archetypal witness to Christ, who inspired the work of the Evangelists, the Apostles, the martyrs and all the saints throughout salvation history. He will always fortify His chosen ones and seek to illumine the unbelievers.

The Holy Spirit must expose the world's sin, especially its denial of Christ.

Nevertheless I tell you the truth: it is to your advantage that I go away, for if I do not go away, the Counselor will not come to you; but if I go, I will send Him to you. And when He comes, He will convince the world of sin and of righteousness and of judgment: of sin, because they do not believe in me; of righteousness, because I go

---

3. *Ex.* 31:1-3.
4. Read more in *Leviticus* 8.
5. *Prov.* 9:1.
6. *John* 15:26.

to the Father, and you will see me no more; of judgment, because the ruler of this world is judged. I have many things to say to you, but you cannot bear them now. When the Spirit of truth comes, He will guide you into all the truth; for He will not speak on His own authority, but whatever He hears He will speak, and He will declare to you the things that are to come. He will glorify me, for He will take what is mine and declare it to you. All that the Father has is mine; therefore I said that He will take what is mine and declare it to you.[7]

Sadly, the place of the Holy Spirit has been denied in the past and continues to be rejected today. Just as Arius denied that Jesus was God, so too did Macedonius and his followers deny that the Holy Spirit was God.

- ### MACEDONIUS DENIED THAT THE HOLY SPIRIT WAS GOD

Macedonius was the bishop of Constantinople from 351 to 360, after the Arians convinced Byzantine Emperor Constantius to place him there because of his Arian tendencies. As such, Macedonius persecuted traditional believers because they believed in the consubstantiality of the Son with the Father. When in the year 360 the emperor was told of the torture, imprisonment and banishment that Macedonius had inflicted in the name of his Arian beliefs, the emperor had him removed and replaced with Eudoxius. Once deposed, Macedonius remained near Constantinople, continued to exacerbate tensions between the Arians and non-Arians, founded his own community and formulated a position against the Holy Spirit similar to what he believed about Jesus: namely, he denied the Trinity as well as the personhood and divinity of the Holy Spirit.

---

7. *John* 16:7-15.

Macedonius based his arguments on two perceptions. First, that the canons about the Holy Spirit, written at the first council at Nicea in 325, were theologically unclear. But, although it is fair to say that the original Creed promulgated at Nicea did not expand much on what was meant by "we believe in the Holy Spirit," the Tradition had always been clear that the Holy Spirit was God and consubstantial with the Father and the Son. Secondly, that *Hebrews* 1:14[8] should be interpreted to mean that the "Holy Spirit," referred to in Scripture is really just *a* spirit of God. This abstraction was based in part on an ancient, pagan Greek belief[9] and essentially reduced the Holy Spirit to one among a multitude of spiritual beings. The result of this heresy was that the followers of Macedonius—called *Pneumatomachi*, meaning "combaters of the Spirit"—speculated that there was a spirit of God, but that spirit was a mere creature, like an angel.

- STS. ATHANASIUS, BASIL, GREGORY OF NYSSA, AND GREGORY OF NAZIANZUS EXPLAIN THE HOLY SPIRIT

This heresy was combated first by St. Athanasius (who, if you recall, also fought vigorously against the Arians), who convoked a local synod in Alexandria in 362 to condemn it. As early as when he was writing against the Arians on the topic of justification, Athanasius had already started making the argument for the consubstantiality of the Spirit with the Father and the Son.

---

8. "Are they not all ministering spirits sent forth to serve, for the sake of those who are to obtain salvation?"

9. The Greek word *daimon* becomes *daemon* in Latin and "demon" in English. While the modern usage of this word means "evil spirit," the ancient Greek term referred to any spiritual being, whether good or bad, that existed somewhere between God and man.

But this is God's kindness to man, that of whom He is Maker, of them according to grace He afterwards becomes Father also; becomes, that is, when men, His creatures, receive into their hearts, as the Apostle says, "the Spirit of his Son, crying, Abba, Father." Arid these are they who, having received the Word, gained power from Him to become sons of God; for they could not become sons, being by nature creatures, otherwise than receiving the Spirit of the natural and true Son. Wherefore, that this might be, "The Word became flesh," that He might make man capable of Godhead.[10]

In quoting St. Paul from Galatians, Athanasius made the point not only that man is justified before God when he takes on the same spirit (that is, the same attributes and attitude) that Jesus took when He humbled Himself in the Garden of Gethsemane, but also that man is justified before God when he takes on the same Spirit—the Holy Spirit—that Jesus had within Him. Because the Holy Spirit is God and because God gives Himself to us freely (ordinarily through the invocation of the Holy Spirit in the Sacraments), man can become more than a creature when he allows the Spirit of God to enter him. The lesson is that, through the Holy Spirit, man can be *deified* in Christ.

Later, and in the specific context of expunging the Macedonian heresy, Athanasius wrote to Serapion to explain that it is a heresy to believe that the Spirit is merely a creature. He made the point that the Trinity is perfection and that removing one part from the whole reduces God.

But if there is such coordination and unity within the holy Triad, who can separate either the Son from the Father, or the Spirit from the Son or from the Father himself? Who would be so audacious as

---

10. Four Discourses Against the Arians, Or 2:59. Philip Schaff, D.D., L.L.D., and Henry Wace, D.D., eds, *Athanasius,* vol. IV of *Nicene and Post-Nicene Fathers of the Christian Church* (New York: Charles Scribner's Sons, 1904), p. 380.

to say that the Triad is unlike itself and diverse in nature, or that the Son is in essence foreign from the Father, or the Spirit alien from the Son? . . . For as the Son, who is in the Father and the Father in him, is not a creature but pertains to the essence of the Father (for this you also profess to say); so also it is not lawful to rank with the creatures the Spirit who is in the Son, and the Son in him, nor to divide him from the Word and reduce the Triad to imperfection.[11]

Over time, the Macedonian heresy continued to grow until Amphilochius of Iconium asked St. Basil the Great to write his seminal work on the Holy Spirit. In one of his key letters on the subject, Basil refuted the idea that the Holy Spirit was a mere creature by comparing the holiness that man can acquire and the holiness that is in the nature of God.

You say that the Holy Spirit is a creature. And every creature is a servant of the Creator, for "all are your servants." If then He is a servant, His holiness is acquired; and everything of which the holiness is acquired is receptive of evil; but the Holy Spirit being holy in essence is called "fount of holiness." Therefore the Holy Spirit is not a creature. If He is not a creature, He is of one of essence and substance with the Father.[12]

His point was that the Holy Spirit is different than other spiritual beings—primarily angels and demons, but also humans—because the Holy Spirit not only was not *given* His holiness (meaning that it pre-existed) but also that He is the fount of holiness. He

---

11. Letter to Serapion, I:20-21. Philip Schaff, D.D., L.L.D., and Henry Wace, D.D., eds, *Athanasius*, vol. IV of *Nicene and Post-Nicene Fathers of the Christian Church* (New York: Charles Scribner's Sons, 1904).

12. Letters, No. 8:10. Philip Schaff, D.D., L.L.D., and Henry Wace, D.D., eds, *Basil*, vol. VIII of *Nicene and Post-Nicene Fathers of the Christian Church*. (New York: Charles Scribner's Sons, 1904), p. 120.

further made the point that only a non-created being can be God, and since the Holy Spirit is holiness itself, then He must be consubstantial with the Father and the Son. In other words: the Holy Spirit is God. Another point He is making is that only creatures can become evil. God in His essence is pure love, pure wisdom, pure holiness. Creatures, by the very fact that their nature is less than that of God's, are by nature capable of doing less than God. Therefore, God (the Holy Spirit in this case) cannot be an evil demon, while mankind can succumb to evil beings.

Basil, in writing to his brother Gregory (also bishop of Nyssa), reaffirmed the point that the Holy Spirit is attached to both the Son and the Father and that the Holy Spirit is known by His work in creation (meaning that all goodness comes from the Holy Spirit). He wrote that this goodness not only encompasses the physical world but encompasses all that man can be as a consequence of creation and the Sacraments. St. Paul writes that as a multiplying effect of the sacramental invocation of the Holy Spirit, certain fruits can be witnessed in creation, such as love, joy, peace, patience, kindness, goodness, faithfulness, gentleness and self-control.[13] Although Basil did not expound on these gifts, he showed how a person can know God first in the manifestation of these gifts and secondly through the interaction with any person of the Trinity. Through reason and illumination, one can experience the division and the unity of the Trinity at once.

He who perceives the Father, and perceives Him by Himself, has at the same time mental perception of the Son; and he who receives the Son does not divide Him from the Spirit, but, in consecution so far as nature is concerned, expresses the faith commingled in himself in the three together. He who makes mention of the Spirit alone, embraces

---

13. *Gal.* 5:22-23.

also in this confession Him of whom He is the Spirit. And since the Spirit is Christ's and of God, as says Paul, then just as he who lays hold on one end of the chain pulls the other to him, so he who "draws the Spirit," as says the prophet, by this means draws to him at the same time both the Son and the Father. And if any one verily receives the Son, he will hold Him on both sides, the Son drawing towards him on the one His own Father, and on the other His own Spirit . . . For it is in no wise possible to entertain the idea of severance or division, in such a way as that the Son should be thought of apart from the Father, or the Spirit be disjoined from the Son. But the communion and the distinction apprehended in Them are, in a certain sense, ineffable and inconceivable, the continuity of nature being never rent asunder by the distinction of the hypostases, nor the notes of proper distinction confounded in the community of essence.[14]

Athanasius made clear that in knowing the Holy Spirit a person can know God in His entirety. Although God is One, His persons are distinctive, and although the persons of the Trinity are distinctive, this does not distort the unity or essence of the Trinity. These classic formulations were meant to confound the Macedonians and others who did not understand the nature and role of the Holy Spirit.

Fourth-century Bishop St. Gregory of Nyssa—the younger brother of Basil the Great—showed that the three persons of the Trinity were all consubstantially God because each shares the works—or energies—of the others.

Every operation which extends from God to the Creation, and is named according to our variable conceptions of it, has its origin from the Father, and proceeds through the Son, and is perfected in the

14. Letters, No. 38 [to his brother Gregory]. Philip Schaff, D.D., L.L.D., and Henry Wace, D.D., eds, Basil, vol. VIII of Nicene and Post-Nicene Fathers of the Christian Church. (New York: Charles Scribner's Sons, 1904), p. 138-9.

Holy Spirit. For this reason the name derived from the operation is not divided in the multitude of operations.[15]

Take note, also, of his point that the names we give for the various operations of God are names we developed. His point in saying this is that God in His inner life—His essence—is truly unknowable. By the illumination of the Holy Spirit, we are able to make some sense of what He has revealed to us about Himself.

And so one who diligently studies the depths of the mystery, receives secretly in his spirit, indeed, a moderate amount of apprehension of the doctrine of God's nature, yet he is unable to explain clearly in words the ineffable depth of this mystery. As, for instance, how the same thing is capable of being numbered and yet rejects numeration, how it is observed with distinctions yet is apprehended as a monad, how it is separate as to personality yet it not divided as to subject matter.[16]

St. Gregory of Nazianzus, a fourth-century archbishop of Constantinople who is considered one of the great Trinitarian theologians of the early Church, wrote about the consubstantiality of the Spirit with the Father and the Son. He specifically defended the ability of the Trinity to be one in nature and three in personhood.

And when I speak of God you must be illumined at once by one flash of light and by three. Three in Individualities or Hypostases, if any prefer so to call them, or persons, for we will not quarrel about names so long as the syllables amount to the same meaning; but one in respect to Substance—that is, the Godhead. For they are divided

---

15. On "Not Three Gods". Philip Schaff, D.D., L.L.D., and Henry Wace, D.D., *eds*, *Gregory of Nyssa*, vol. V of *Nicene and Post-Nicene Fathers of the Christian Church*. (New York: Charles Scribner's Sons, 1904), p. 334.

16. The Great Catechism. Philip Schaff, D.D., L.L.D., and Henry Wace, D.D., *eds*, *Gregory of Nyssa*, vol. V of *Nicene and Post-Nicene Fathers of the Christian Church*. (New York: Charles Scribner's Sons, 1904), p. 403.

without division, if I may so say; and they are united in division. For the Godhead is one in three, and the three are one, in whom the Godhead is one in three, and the three are one, in whom the Godhead is, or to speak more accurately, Who are the Godhead.[17]

As a direct result of the work these early theologians completed on the matter of the Holy Spirit, within the tradition there was agreement on the theology of the Holy Spirit. By the time the Second Ecumenical Council was convoked in Constantinople in 381, there was a decision to amend the Nicene Creed promulgated in 325. The section of the Creed on the Holy Spirit was changed to read as follows: "And in the Holy Spirit, the Lord and Giver of Life, who proceeds from the Father,[18] who with the Father and the Son together is worshiped and glorified, who has spoken through the prophets."

- ### Heresies against the Holy Spirit are Particularly Blasphemous

It is interesting to note here that there was a minor tradition which proclaimed that committing a heresy against the Holy Spirit is worse than committing one against Jesus Christ. It was, in part, based on the Gospel of *Matthew*.

---

17. Orations, No. 39. Philip Schaff, D.D., L.L.D., and Henry Wace, D.D., *eds, Gregory of Nazianzen,* vol. VII of *Nicene and Post-Nicene Fathers of the Christian Church.* (New York: Charles Scribner's Sons, 1904), p. 355.

18. Keep in mind that leftover concerns about Arianism in the West are partly responsible for the schism between West and East. One result of certain local councils in the West was an alteration of the original Nicene-Constantinopolitan Creed. In the third section of the Creed on the origins of the Holy Spirit, the original text read "who proceeds from the Father." These councils added the phrase "and the Son" (*filioque*) after that so it would read "who proceeds from the Father and the Son."

He who is not with me is against me, and he who does not gather with me scatters. Therefore I tell you, every sin and blasphemy will be forgiven men, but the blasphemy against the Spirit will not be forgiven. And whoever says a word against the Son of man will be forgiven; but whoever speaks against the Holy Spirit will not be forgiven, either in this age or in the age to come.[19]

This earliest tradition held that because the Second Person of the Trinity came as a unity of God and man, that it was understandable that this reality caused some confusion. Therefore, in some small way, heresies against Jesus are more understandable because of His unique nature. In contrast, since the Holy Spirit is the pure Spirit of God (without the addition of a human nature, human will, etc.), there is less confusion about Him than there is about Christ.

Thus, not only are heresies against the Third Person of the Trinity less tolerable, but they also reveal the heart of a person that is persistently hardened.

- NEW AGE AND ENVIRONMENTAL MOVEMENTS EMBRACE A NEO-PAGAN UNIVERSALISM

Today, man persists in this hardness of heart. He sought in the twentieth century to put Himself above God and to ignore the work of the Holy Spirit. Equally as heinous as the wars that plagued our civilization during that time were the movements, clothed in the language of peace, that have torn humanity away from the one God who lovingly and wisely remains in our midst as the Holy Spirit.

The New Age movement is a prime example of how a combination of Enlightenment humanism, spiritual division and

---

19. *Matt.* 12:30-32.

confusion, and the occult have joined forces not only to reject Scripture and Tradition but also the divine personhood of Jesus the Christ and His Holy Spirit. New Age spirituality, which gripped the United States from the mid-1960s through the 1970s and into the early 1980s, sought to collect elements of cosmology, astrology, occultism, esotericism, pantheism, Kabbalah and some of the polytheistic tendencies of Asian religions into a loosely configured philosophical paradigm. By co-opting aspects of wellness (yoga, meditation), health care (alternative medicine), psychology, literature, economics, politics, environmentalism and entertainment, this so-called postmodern holistic movement injected itself into every aspect of society. With the tacit approval of the elites on university campuses and in the media, America was flooded with a neo-pagan universalism that penetrated the political system and restructured society away from its Judeo-Christian roots, in part by rejecting Scripture, Tradition, authority and doctrines like the Trinity as outmoded ways of thinking.

The utopian cosmological, astrological and psychological influences of the New Age movement encouraged a kind of spiritual experimentation that sought to explain the spiritual realm in ways that reduced traditional religion to man-made structures of oppression. In so doing—no surprise to those who recognize the Judas Syndrome at work—the New Age movement was precisely Macedonian in its attempt to reduce the Holy Spirit to one among many spiritual beings. "God," for those that embraced this manner of thinking, was not just everywhere but every*thing*; unabashed pantheism perpetuated a rejection of the unity of God and the specificity of the Holy Spirit as a divine person within the Godhead.

In recent years, New Age ideology has coalesced around the environmentalist movement. The Church has long held that Creation is the gift of God to man and that man has a responsibility of stewardship towards it, but the religion of modern environmentalism replaces Christian doctrine with an emotionalism that clouds reason and marginalizes the real illumination provided to us by the Holy Spirit. However necessary—even praiseworthy—it is for people to love and protect animals, air, water and land, it is not permissible in the process to conflate God with the natural hierarchy. In co-opting the pantheistic tendencies of the New Age movement, environmentalism not only alienates large swaths of Christians who otherwise favor environmental stewardship, but explicitly antagonizes them by presenting a false dichotomy between traditional Christianity and "saving the planet."

As if this wasn't bad enough, some environmentalists in America today try to make radical environmental policy a shibboleth for Christian faith, invoking, for instance, the "What Would Jesus Do?" slogan to seduce the young and the misinformed. Like all heretics, they aim to confuse and guilt communities into reshaping their understanding of and commitment to values like love and responsibility. This twisting of vital Christian concepts in order to implement radical political agendas is particularly troubling.

• Reductionist Spiritualities in the Church

Because too many Catholic leaders were caught up in the rampant liberalism that characterized the decades following World War II, they inadvertently (in most cases) encouraged a kind of practical Macedonianism throughout parishes in the United States. Within the context of so-called social justice movements, catechists adopted the language of the New Age movement, bombarding believers with questions about how religion made them "feel," inviting them to explore alternative spiritualities that often had their roots in Asian meditation, urging them to become unduly involved in Church governance, and encouraging them to diversify their religious expression to the point of indifferentism and syncretism. Believers have been led to sacrifice their understanding of the Triune God for what they would say is an equally legitimate spiritual paradigm. Since the role of the Holy Spirit can often be harder to understand, the tendency has been to turn the Holy Spirit into a type of guardian angel, which, of course, is the heresy that Macedonius started.

The worst part about these efforts is that they were all-too-often clothed in the language of Scripture, giving them a false air of orthodoxy and authority. There was also an aspect of guilt implanted in them, because the simplified language set up a false juxtaposition between believers who were focused on social justice or interior conversion over and against those focused on liturgy, the Sacraments, and other externals of faithful practice.

A kind of practical Macedonianism can also be witnessed in the way some religious symbols have been adapted for church use. Ignoring the dictates of Scripture and Tradition, parishes began using too many symbols of creation to explain God: for example, the use of natural elements like fountains with rocks to express the new life of Baptism, or tabernacles built to resemble a carpenter's tool box. The metaphorical use of God's creation communicated to believers a type of theology and spirituality that reduced God to the profane things of the world, exuding a type of pantheism expressive of the Holy Spirit's creature-hood as taught by Macedonius and his followers.

Without the Holy Spirit at the Epiphany, the world would not have known of the Incarnation of Jesus, and without the Holy Spirit at Pentecost the world would not have known about the saving grace of the Crucifixion or the Resurrection. Despite recognizing that God communicated Himself to man in this way, Macedonius chose to ignore the divinity of the Holy Spirit and also encouraged others to develop for themselves a pagan faith made up of mythical spirits who can be worshiped and conjured for our use and benefit. In a way, Macedonius became a bridge between the ancient pagan world and our post-Christian time. For modern man to ignore the divinity of the Holy Spirit or to ignore His unique role within the Holy Trinity is to commit a grave sin, not only against dogma but also against the plan God has for all mankind. It is vitally important to understand that this Spirit not only teaches us about Christ but urgently ushers us toward our eschatological end in the Kingdom of God in Heaven.

CHAPTER SEVEN

Origenism
Ignoring the Just Judgment

G OD, OUT OF LOVE, has always hoped for the return of His people, and out of wisdom, He has given us everything we need to return to Him. From the moment of our creation, our Father in Heaven has been there supporting us in life. God the Spirit has filled the Church and its people with every possible grace and blessing so that we would know we were called to live with God for eternity. It is Christ who is the sheepfold, the gate through which we enter the Kingdom of our Father. He is the just judge who will identify us individually and collectively, whether we merit eternal reward or eternal damnation. We should take great solace in this, because the mercy of God is abundant and His love is unfolding evermore.

Origen, who in many ways was a praiseworthy early churchman, went a step too far theologically by proposing that damnation was not eternal, the reason being that God allowed further growth and improvement after death. Today, modern secularism approaches the question of the afterlife not with theological imprecisions but with a visceral incredulity. This is due, in part, to the habit of progressives who have tried to convince each generation that a person owes nothing to anyone except himself. The net effect of such a belief system, of course, is that the question of eternal reward or damnation has been relegated to the margins of modern thinking.

On the one hand there are those who propose that the afterlife is not a reality worth considering, and on the other hand there are those who have become obsessed with it. Sadly, the problem of indifference has crept into the Church through myriad priests and religious who have whitewashed questions about the four final things: death, judgment, Heaven and Hell.

- GOD'S JUDGING CHARACTER IN THE OLD TESTAMENT

At the Second Coming of Christ, all mankind will again appear before Christ in the collective judgment to give an account of how faithful to the will of God humanity has been. At that time, all will be joined with or separated from God like the proverbial sheep and goats. As the Psalmist indicates below, God rules the universe as the eternal high priest who not only loves and protects His flock, but also as the just judge who watches our love and commitment for Him.

> For Thou hast maintained my just cause; Thou hast sat on the throne giving righteous judgment. Thou hast rebuked the nations, Thou hast destroyed the wicked; Thou hast blotted out their name for ever and ever . . . But the Lord sits enthroned for ever, He has established His throne for judgment; and He judges the world with righteousness, He judges the peoples with equity . . . The Lord has made Himself known, He has executed judgment; the wicked are snared in the work of their own hands . . . Arise, O Lord! Let not man prevail; let the nations be judged before Thee! Put them in fear, O Lord! Let the nations know that they are but men![1]

Take note, too, of the last verse in the above passage. The Psalmist understands that we must be reminded we are mere mortals. He

---

1. *Ps.* 9:4-5, 7-8, 16, 19-20.

knows we are arrogant and weak and that we must humble ourselves before God. And because we seem to find a way to drown
in sin and filth generation after generation, God offers us His
wisdom so that we can learn what is right in His eyes, and He
gives us the tools to judge our actions along the way.

> With Thee is wisdom, who knows Thy works and was present when
> Thou didst make the world, and who understand what is pleasing in
> Thy sight and what is right according to Thy commandments. Send
> her forth from the holy heavens, and from the throne of Thy glory
> send her, that she may be with me and toil, and that I may learn what
> is pleasing to Thee.[2]

As we stand before God today and ask Him to assist us in our
labors, let us not forget that when our ancestors did the same
thing they included in their worship a healthy fear of God. We
should do more of that these days, because it helps us to remain in
proper relationship to God. More than that, it helps us to keep a
better handle on what enormous gifts God is already giving to us
to prepare for the life to come.

> The fear of the Lord is glory and exultation, and gladness and a crown
> of rejoicing. The fear of the lord delights the heart, and gives glad-
> ness and joy and long life. With him who fears the Lord it will go
> well at the end; on the day of his death he will be blessed. To fear the
> Lord is the beginning of wisdom; she is created with the faithful in
> the womb. She made among men an eternal foundation, and among
> their descendents she be trusted.[3]

They knew then, as we should be reminded today, that without
fear we can never truly appreciate how intimate God is with us.

---

2. *Wis.* 9:9-10.
3. *Sirach* 1:11-15.

That may seem strange at first, but fear can be a powerful tool that leads to humility, which leads to virtue and ultimately our salvation. God is not trying to scare us, for sure, but we cannot honestly say we are placing ourselves in His care if we are not also supplicating ourselves in service to the Father over and against the worship of mankind.

King Nebuchadnezzar's experience in *Daniel* 4:4-8 is not only proof enough of God's desire to humble the proud but an example of how we must take seriously His warnings to us about the greater calamities that may befall us. In the case of Nebuchadnezzar, it was only the prophet Daniel, with the Spirit of God in him, who could help the king understand what the one, true God was communicating. God was trying to explain to our ancestors that the worst possible material condemnation for man is death. Since death is only an end to the physical world, it is not the worst possible result for the totality of man. "And do not fear those who kill the body but cannot kill the soul; rather fear him who can destroy both soul and body in hell."[4]

- God Judges with Love and Mercy in the New Testament

The choices we make in life matter. That is why God communicated to us that we cannot be concerned merely with our earthly life but that the life after death matters too. That is one reason why God becomes incarnate. He knew we would get distracted by the things of the earth and sent Himself to steer us back to our eternal life.

> And if you invoke as Father Him who judges each one impartially according to his deeds, conduct yourselves with fear throughout the

---

4. *Matt.* 10:28.

time of your exile. You know that you were ransomed from the futile ways inherited from your fathers, not with perishable things such as silver or gold, but with the precious blood of Christ, like that of a lamb without blemish or spot.[5]

Understanding our inheritance makes it all the more vital to repair and improve our lives in the here and now by understanding that we must make a choice for or against God. We cannot remain neutral in the fight between good and evil. "I know your works: you are neither cold not hot. Would that you were cold or hot! So, because you are lukewarm, and neither cold nor hot, I will spew you out of my mouth."[6]

Our lives, therefore, should be lived in accordance with God's will not because we owe some kind of payment or sacrifice to make us pleasing before God, but rather as the means of living through Him, with Him and in Him. "He was destined before the foundation of the world but was made manifest at the end of the times for your sake. Through Him you have confidence in God, who raised Him from the dead and gave Him glory, so that your faith and hope are in God."[7] This is the overall thrust of our judgment before the throne of love and wisdom. In other words, we will be judged in part on our belief, on our trust in God, on how we followed God's will in our lives, and how much we allowed ourselves to go on the journey of deification.

"When the Son of Man comes in His glory, and all the angels with Him, then He will sit on His glorious throne. Before Him will be gathered all the nations, and He will separate them one from another

---

5. *1 Ptr.* 1:17-19.
6. *Rev.* 3:15-16.
7. *1 Ptr.* 1:20-21.

as a shepherd separates the sheep from the goats, and He will place the sheep at His right hand, but the goats at the left."[8]

The sheep will be those who followed these guidelines for living in the Lord, and the goats will be those who rejected Him all along the way.

• ORIGEN DENIED THAT HELL IS ETERNAL

Many apostates, of course, have denied the importance of the Judgment. There are also, however, occasions in the history of the Church where otherwise faithful and committed theologians have made mistakes in their understanding of Christ's individual and collective judgment. One such man was Origen, who was born in 185, saw his first Roman persecution by the time he was 17 years old, and as a young man gained a reputation for being a powerful preacher. Origen made his way to Antioch and Greece, and somewhere around 218 he was ordained a priest. By 231, he had begun disagreeing with his bishop in Alexandria and was banished to Caesarea in Palestine, which allowed him to serve under his protector and friend Theoctistus.

A prolific writer, Origen penned many influential documents that were used as sources by some of the earliest Church Fathers: his theology and commentaries on Scripture in particular. The reason Origen came under the suspicion and scrutiny of the Church was that it appeared that he proposed a theory of man's final destination that contradicted Scripture and the early Tradition. Essentially, Origen proposed that at the end of time all of humanity would be saved, that even the devil himself would be redeemed; this is a concept called *apokatastasis* or universal redemption.

---

8. *Matt.* 25:31-33.

The end of the world, then, and the final consummation, will take place when every one shall be subjected to punishment for his sins; a time which God alone knows, when He will bestow on each one what he deserves. We think, indeed, that the goodness of God, through his Christ, may recall all His creatures to one end, even His enemies being conquered and subdued.[9]

Although the third and fourth centuries are often considered as an age of eschatological optimism, even for his time Origen went too far. Other churchmen of the age *hoped* all men would be saved, but Origen went so far as to write that all men *would* be saved. Origen confirms his belief in *apokatastasis* in a passage detailing the resurrection of the body. It is important here to take note of how he refers to a process of purification after death: that there are cycles after death, and the final "time" will come when all have been transformed.

Into this condition, then, we are to suppose that all this bodily substance of ours will be brought, when all things shall be re-established in a state of unity, and when God shall be all in all. And this result must be understood as being brought about, not suddenly, but slowly and gradually, seeing that the process of amendment and correction will take place imperceptibly in the individual instances during the lapse of countless and unmeasured ages, some outstripping others, and tending by a swifter course towards perfection, while others again follow close at hand, and some again a long way behind; and this, through the numerous and uncounted orders of progressive being who are being

---

9. On First Principles, book one, chapter six. The Rev. Alexander Roberts, D.D. and James Donaldson, LL.D., *eds, Origen*, vol. IV of *The Anti-Nicene Fathers. Translations of the Writings of the Fathers down to A.D. 325* American reprint of the Edinburgh edition. Revised and chronologically arranged with brief prefaces and occasional notes by A. Cleveland Coxe, D.D. (New York: Charles Scribner's Sons, 1899).

reconciled to God from a state of enmity, the last enemy is finally reached, who is called death, so that he also may be destroyed, and no longer be an enemy. When therefore, all rational souls shall have been restored to a condition of this kind, then the nature of this body of ours will undergo a change into the glory of a spiritual body.[10]

The Church saw in Origen a contradiction to Scripture[11] on the question of judgment and of the eternity of Hell. Consider the unquenchable fire mentioned in *Mark* 9:43. Eternal punishment is also a key theme in *Matthew*, including passages about the fires of Hell (5:22), the sending away of evildoers (25:41, 7:23 and 25:13), and the promise that "they will go away into eternal punishment, but the righteous into eternal life."[12] St. John, in referring to the necessity of believing in Jesus Christ, wrote: "He who believes in Him is not condemned; he who does not believe is condemned already, because he has not believed in the name of the only Son of God."[13] St. Paul wrote: "For we must all appear before the judgment seat of Christ, so that each one may receive good or evil, according to what he has done in the body."[14] And in *Revelation*, St. John wrote, "and if any one's name was not found written in the book of life, he was thrown into the lake of fire."[15]

The Church also saw that Origen had not separated himself enough from the pagan philosophy that had influenced him so

---

10. *On First Principles*, book three, chapter six. The Rev. Alexander Roberts, D.D. and James Donaldson, LL.D., *eds, Origen*, vol. IV of *The Anti-Nicene Fathers. Translations of the Writings of the Fathers down to A.D. 325.* American reprint of the Edinburgh edition. Revised and chronologically arranged with brief prefaces and occasional notes by A. Cleveland Coxe, D.D. (New York: Charles Scribner's Sons, 1899), p. 345.

11. It should be noted that in Origen's life the canon of Scripture had not been fully promulgated yet.

12. *Matt.* 25:46.

13. *John* 3:18.

14. *2 Cor.* 5:10.

15. *Rev.* 20:15.

much. The ancient Greeks speculated that improvement or pro-
gression was not limited to a person's earthly life. Instead, they
posited that even after death a person could learn and grow until
he reached a state of blessedness. Origen concluded that, until all
people gain this state of blessedness, there will not be a final consummation of the universe.

The net effect of the influence of Origen's theology—that all
men *will* be saved—was that believers embraced the idea that
there was no need for a sense of urgency in their spiritual life
and, therefore, no need for an urgency to get into the Church or
to rush toward the Sacraments. The connection, of course, was
that if one wasn't worried about what was going to become of his
afterlife, then he wouldn't worry about his actions in this life. In
witnessing this dangerous attitude among their flocks, the Fathers
of the Ecumenical Council of Second Constantinople in 553 condemned Origen's writing on *apokatastasis* within the larger body
of his work.

- STS. JOHN OF DAMASCUS, GREGORY OF NYSSA AND
  GREGORY OF NAZIANZEN EXPLAIN JUDGMENT

Some saints and theologians, such as John of Damascus, Gregory
of Nyssa and Gregory of Nazianzen, were similar to Origen in
that they too were reluctant to subscribe to an eschatology that
included man's ultimate rejection of or eternal separation from
God. However, as optimistic as they were, these men of faith
never denied that Hell was a real possibility.

We shall therefore rise again, our souls being once more united with
our bodies, now made incorruptible and having put off corruption,
and we shall stand beside the awful judgment-seat of Christ; and the
devil and his demons and the man that is his, that is the Antichrist

and the impious and the sinful, will be given over to everlasting fire: not material fire like our fire, but such fire as God would know. But those who have done good will shine forth as the sun with the angels into life eternal, with our Lord Jesus Christ, ever seeing Him and being in His sight and deriving unceasing joy from Him, praising Him with the Father and the Holy Spirit throughout the limitless ages of ages.[16]

Not only is Hell considered to be eternal, but this Hell is considered to be a place of torment unlike any physical torment known to man.

For I know a cleansing fire which Christ came to send upon the earth, and He Himself is anagogically called a Fire ... I know also a fire which is not cleansing, but avenging; either that fire of Sodom which He pours down on all sinners, mingled with brimstone and storms, or that which is prepared for the Devil and His Angels or that which proceeds from the face of the Lord, and shall burn up his enemies round about; and one even more fearful still than these, the unquenchable fire which is ranged with the worm that dies not but is eternal for the wicked. For all these belong to the destroying power; though some may prefer even in this place to take a more merciful view of this fire, worthily of Him that chastises.[17]

Our ancestors in the faith knew back then, and teach us now, that the punishments experienced in Hell are real and not metaphorical.

---

16. Exposition of the Orthodox Faith, Bk. 4, Ch. 27. Philip Schaff, D.D., L.L.D., and Henry Wace, D.D., eds, *John of Damascus*, vol. IX of *Nicene and Post-Nicene Fathers of the Christian Church.* (New York: Charles Scribner's Sons, 1904), p. 101.

17. Orations 40:36. Philip Schaff, D.D., L.L.D., and Henry Wace, D.D., eds, *Gregory of Nazianzen*, vol. VII of *Nicene and Post-Nicene Fathers of the Christian Church.* (New York: Charles Scribner's Sons, 1904), p. 373.

Indeed, the sinner's life of torment presents no equivalent to anything that pains the sense here. Even if some one of the punishments in that other world be named in terms that are well known here, the distinction is still not small. When you hear the word fire, you have been taught to think of a fire other than the fire we see, owing to something being added to that fire which in this there is not; for that fire is never quenched, whereas experience has discovered many ways of quenching this; and there is a great difference between a fire which can be extinguished, and one that does not admit of extinction.[18]

The Church Fathers taught that it was better to be reproved now than at the time of the judgment. Since our lives have been distorted and disrupted by how we live, the experience of sin and evil gives us a chance to come closer to Christ. This is, in part, why belief and participation in the Sacraments are so vital. Through them, we are more capable of battling our own sins from within and the evil that comes to us from without. Not to mention, of course, it is better to be reproved now, because after death there is no more chance to gain the grace of God.

I know the emptying, the making void, the making waste, the melting of the heart, and knocking of the knees together, such are the punishments of the ungodly. I do not dwell on the judgments to come, to which indulgence in this world delivers us, as it is better to be punished and cleansed now than to be transmitted to the torment to come, when it is the time of chastisement, not of cleansing.[19]

---

18. The Great Catechism, Ch. 40. Philip Schaff, D.D., L.L.D., and Henry Wace, D.D., eds, *Gregory of Nyssa*, vol. V of *Nicene and Post-Nicene Fathers of the Christian Church*. (New York: Charles Scribner's Sons, 1904), p. 508-09.

19. Orations 16:7. Philip Schaff, D.D., L.L.D., and Henry Wace, D.D., eds, *Gregory of Nazianzen*, vol. VII of *Nicene and Post-Nicene Fathers of the Christian Church*. (New York: Charles Scribner's Sons, 1904), p. 249.

When the believer faithfully follows Jesus Christ, the fearful experience of evil and sin is transformed into acts of love and obedience. In this way, the believer may look forward to death. In addition, however, we believe that our prayers for the dead are effective in God's eternity. Even though we do not believe people can willingly change after death, we do believe our prayers assist sinners before the judgment seat of Christ. In this way, believers have the confidence that even unbelievers will have hope in death.

Weep for the unbelievers; weep for those who differ in nowise from them, those who depart hence without the illumination, without the seal! They indeed deserve our wailing, they deserve our groans, they are outside the Palace, with the culprits, with the condemned: for "verily I say unto you, except a man be born of water and the Spirit, he shall not enter into the kingdom of Heaven." Mourn for those who have died in wealth and did not from their wealth think of any solace for their soul, who had power to wash away their sins and would not . . . Let us weep for these; let us assist them according to our power; let us think of some assistance for them, small though it be, yet still let us assist them. How and in what way? By praying and entreating others to make prayers for them, by continually giving to the poor on their behalf . . . Not in vain did the Apostles order that remembrance should be made of the dead in the dreadful Mysteries. They know that great gain results to them, great benefit; for when the whole people stands with uplifted hands, a priestly assembly, and that awful Sacrifice lies displayed, how shall we not prevail with God by our entreaties for them. And this we do for those who have departed in faith.[20]

---

20. Homilies on Philippians, 3:4. Philip Schaff, D.D., L.L.D., and Henry Wace, D.D., *eds, John Chrysostom*, vol. XIII of *Nicene and Post-Nicene Fathers of the Christian Church*. (New York: Charles Scribner's Sons, 1904), p. 197.

These Church Fathers drew out the larger point: that the question about judgment in the New Testament comes down to whether or not we make a choice for life and goodness or death and evil. Even though hope is in abundance because of the Crucifixion and Resurrection, we cannot be saved against our own will, meaning that hope can neither save us from what we choose to believe nor from how we choose to act.

- ### Secularism Denies Accountability in the Life to Come

Rampant secularism in the Western world is the best example of a social and political movement that—while not having a specific face because it is made up of people who generally subscribe to a radical separation of church and state, of religion from society and of science from faith—has influenced society not only away from God in general but also from God as a just judge who holds in front of us the real possibility of eternal damnation in Hell or eternal reward in Heaven. Drawing upon ancient Stoic, Epicurean and Averroistic philosophies, as well as the writings of John Locke, James Madison, Thomas Jefferson, Thomas Paine and a variety of agnostics and atheists, the proponents of this general disposition categorically and creatively deny truth by expressing skepticism about orthodoxy, tradition and authority.

Secularism has played itself into a cultural norm in the United States. The entertainment industry in America is thoroughly secularist; the figures who dominate our movie and TV screens disavow "organized" religion and dismiss those who believe that their behavior on earth will be reflected in their life after death. Our shows and films regularly take mean-spirited, derogatory and degrading positions against traditional religion, mocking authority and the Sacraments along the way. The entertainment business does not seem to mind hijacking eschatological themes (death, judgment, Heaven and Hell) when it will make them money, of course, but they do not treat such themes with sincerity and respect.

Likewise, although America has never been and never will be a theocracy, its leaders have traditionally shown respect for Christians. In recent times, however, the political realm has become increasingly antagonistic toward faith. We take for granted now the ludicrous precept that an elected official's political judgments should not be impacted by his personal religious views on serious moral questions such as abortion. We witness time and again politicians who exercise their voting rights based on a set of divine principles being singled out for shame in the public sphere or specially targeted for defeat.

The direct connection between secularism and Origenism comes into focus when we consider a person's general disposition toward faith, public life and judgment after death. If you find that a person is generally not moved by considering his end—meaning his eternal disposition in relationship to God—then he will be generally disposed to taking nihilistic positions because he doesn't see any consequence to his actions. If a person is generally predisposed to believing his actions on earth matter to God and in the life to come, he is more generally disposed to behave in line with Church teaching. This is, in part, what happened to Judas. He was more concerned about the works and judgments of men in this world, instead of being occupied with the will of God and the judgment that is to come in the next.

The passages about Judas's betrayal are challenging because they do not provide us with enough material to piece together an entire picture of his life. They also do not give us enough information to answer the question of why he would betray Jesus, even after knowing Him personally throughout the course of His earthly ministry. This lack of information explains why in literature Judas is often depicted as having committed so many different sins, from greed and pride to envy and wrath. He is portrayed as a thief, a zealot, a political operative, an opportunist, or as one possessed by the devil.

One portrayal of Judas that should more often be noted is from Franco Zeffirelli's 1977 film, *Jesus of Nazareth*. Its Judas is not unappealing. He is a good-looking, well-educated man who acted as if he genuinely thought he had Jesus' best interests at heart. The problem, however, is that he is even more interested in the approval of the powerful, the connected and the wealthy. Even though he was taught that the beginning of the consummation of the world began in the coming of God in flesh, he ignores what he knows in favor of earthly cares and pleasures. In front of the elitists of the community, he never stands up for his original belief that Jesus was the Messiah.

Understanding Judas in this way is important because modern secularism is an almost ubiquitous mode of thinking; it has gripped college campuses, spread to public schools, can be found across the political spectrum and has changed the mores in the workplace. Americans have been programmed to be like Zeffirelli's portrait of Judas, encouraged to live their lives as polished, good-looking, well-educated, financially successful, well-regarded "successes." On their own, these characteristics may not be evil or even objectionable, but taken together they point to the epidemic wherein Christians have fallen asleep in the ether of socially-engineered, middle-class expectations.

- CHRISTIAN SECULARISM AND INDIFFERENCE
  TOWARD JUDGMENT

Christian churches tainted by secularism have exacerbated the problem by basing their doctrine on trends and polling data rather than on the entirety of the Faith, including the consequences for what we believe and how we act. The preachers in evangelical megachurches, for example, make much of their fire and brimstone lectures, but the majority of their sermons focus on man himself. You'll know what I mean if you've seen any of their television commercials or billboards. For starters, the advertising generally focuses on the preacher, which is often a good indication that the life of that community is centered on the personality of the leader rather than on Christ or the community. To follow, the message of the advertising tends to picture the preacher as a blissful person talking about what God wants for *you*. That's a pretty good indication that if you joined his community, you could develop a personal version of Christianity based on your own emotional state of happiness: an approach to God that is selfish and individualistic. These pastors have allowed their flocks to create for themselves a personal faith that could only be described as a Christian Resurrectionism: a Christianity that has no consequences, only personal profit; no judgment or Hell, only good news.

Connected to this are the megachurches that preach what is known as the Prosperity Gospel, which suggests that Jesus wants your material happiness as much as He wants your spiritual or eternal fulfillment, that each person has a God-given right to be prosperous *here on earth*. The leaders of these megachurches seem more interested in motivating people to adjust their attitude as a means of increasing their wallet size, rather than avoiding eternal damnation. This is unabashed secularism wrapped in Scripture verses: the Judas Syndrome at work seducing Christians into denying that the end will eventually come and that each person will have to account for his behavior in front of the judgment seat of Christ.

A further and even more distressing signal of Origenism's resurfacing in the guise of modern secularism is the reluctance (or inability) of Catholic priests to teach and to preach about the realities that await us in death. It is understandable that homilists might prefer to talk of the joyous possibility that God may save everyone in humanity—even the devil himself. It is also understandable how a priest, deacon or theologian could become enamored with the idea of universal redemption by misinterpreting Scripture. As a doctrine, however, *apokatastasis* has been roundly and consistently rejected by Tradition and has also demonstrated itself to be a weak foundation for catechesis when teaching about death, judgment, Heaven and Hell, whereas gently explaining the individual and collective judgments can be used as a loving tool for encouraging discernment about God's will and about how each of us relates to the kingdom of God.

When the Church speaks of the reign of God in earthly terms, it means to say that God so loved us that He created us and later walked among us in the person of Jesus. The earthly kingdom consists, therefore, in doing what Jesus did: feeding the hungry, clothing the naked, fighting for the oppressed, helping the poor, and more. In these activities, we model Christ for each other. The heavenly kingdom also means that God's love and wisdom carry us toward an eschatological end where we directly experience Jesus. Hope in this heavenly kingdom tells us that we are not limited to the sociocultural and political world, but that we are called to step beyond it into communion with God. This is why, in part, we believe in the idea of *deification*, in the supernatural gift that makes it possible for us to grow more like God and to commune with Him after our natural death.

Knowing all of this, then, it might be possible to say that Origen was deficient when it came to understanding the possibilities open to man on earth. Maybe that is why he had to create a device—universal redemption—that made it possible for God to give us one final safety net. Perhaps Origen could not see clearly enough that God already gave us the safety net, by explaining to us what is right and what is wrong through Scripture and the spiritual tradition. Perhaps Origen could not see that God had already given us the tools (the Sacraments) to know how to go about becoming more like Him. Frankly, we know it is possible to grow like and in God because we have the examples of all the saints and the eyewitness testimony of those who witnessed the Transfiguration and the Resurrection. More than that, we have our own living testimony, which partakes of the Eucharist—the living Body and Blood of Jesus Christ offered to us as pure gift out of love and free communication.

CHAPTER EIGHT

Messalianism
Abandoning the Sacraments

IN UNDERSTANDING WHAT LACKS in man, God gave us His Church and its Sacraments in order for us to participate in His divine life. As God is both transcendent (meaning that He is utterly beyond the world and man) and immanent (meaning He makes Himself known to us in an intimate way), it is perfectly logical that He would provide to us the means by which we would know Him and anticipate our return to Him in His kingdom to come. This is supposed to be the driving force behind our spiritual life.

The Messalians, who coalesced in Northern Africa sometime around the year 360, denied the necessity of participating in God's Church or His Sacraments. This renegade group was known for its belief that the human soul contained both a good and an evil spirit. This dualistic manner of thinking led them to believe that the only hope for mankind was a life filled with ecstatic prayer and unencumbered by ecclesiastical authority and discipline, Sacraments (particularly Baptism), and even manual labor. Committed to the ecstatic utterances of their leaders—Adelphius, Symeon and others—they believed they could commune directly with God.

Although the heresy of Messalianism was condemned by the Ecumenical Council at Ephesus in 431, it has reappeared in the prevailing modern American attitude that generic "spirituality" is to be preferred over specific "religion." Adherents of this philosophy of the spiritual life seek a kind of transcendence that is individual-based, emotion-centered and separate from a community. They reject the true faith in Jesus Christ, which must always be corporate, unified, codified and external as well as internal. Elements of this heresy can also be found among the Buddhists, the Quakers, the Pentecostals and certain churchmen who promote an approach to spirituality that diminishes the role of the Church and Sacraments in the spiritual life.

- GOD POINTS MAN TOWARD THE SACRAMENTS IN THE OLD TESTAMENT

The role of the Church and the Sacraments in the spiritual life is pre-figured in the Old Testament. For example, *Psalm* 147 explains how the Father is building Jerusalem, which means He is building a Church for *us*. In doing so, He makes it possible for us to know that He can be found in the world and that we can share in His life through the Sacraments, which are the means of our salvation. In *Psalm* 147, God sends forth His Word (Jesus), who heals the broken-hearted and binds up their wounds, makes the wind blow and the water flow (both in creation and by the Holy Spirit), is strengthening the gates (of the Church), and filling us with wheat (the Eucharist).

Another example of God's preparing to build up a Church and provide us with the Sacraments comes at the end of the second chapter (verses 22-32) of *Joel*. There is a reference to the tree which bore the most fruit (prefiguring the tree that would become the Cross). The vine and fig tree in those verses are about Christ and the Church, while the rain, wheat, wine and oil refer to the food that is best for mankind. In other words, these are references to the matter used in the Sacraments of initiation: water for Baptism, wheat and wine for Eucharist, and oil for anointing in Confirmation (or Chrismation in the Eastern churches) and Ordination. Peter quotes *Joel* 3 on Pentecost in *Acts* 2:17-21. He uses the words of the prophet to show their fulfillment in the building up of the Church (not just the city of Jerusalem) and emphasizing its role in the just judgment: primarily by helping mankind partake of the Sacraments.

Going beyond these general statements in the Old Testament about God's providing us with a Church and Sacraments to assist us on our road back to Him, there are specific passages that point to the Sacraments themselves. For our purposes here, we will not look at every Sacrament, but only those that belong to our initiation in the Church (Baptism, Confirmation and the Eucharist) and to Ordination, because it acts as a guarantor for truth. First is Baptism:

I will greatly rejoice in the Lord, my soul shall exult in my God; for He has clothed me with the garments of salvation, He has covered me with the robe of righteousness, as a bridegroom decks himself with a garland, and as a bride adorns herself with her jewels. For as the earth brings forth its shoots, and as a garden causes what is sown in it to spring up, so the Lord will cause righteousness and praise.[1]

The references here are fairly clear. The garment referred to in this passage is the garment of salvation, which is Christ. In Baptism we put on Christ, as St. Paul writes in *Galatians* 3:27. Of course, when we are baptized, God also causes us to grow.

The second passage we will look at comes from *Ecclesiastes* chapter nine. The verse in this passage that refers to putting "oil

---

1. *Is.* 61:10-11

on your head" is a clear reference to the anointing that comes during Confirmation or Ordination.

> Go, eat your bread with enjoyment, and drink your wine with a merry heart; for God has already approved what you do. Let your garments be always white; let not oil be lacking on your head.[2]

Although the above passage also contains a Eucharistic type by suggesting we should be happy about eating the bread of life and drinking the cup of blessing, there is an additional passage that further suggests that the Eucharist should become a way of life. In the book of *Wisdom*, there is a reference to the people who will become holy if they partake of holy things. This is not merely a general reference to prayer and spirituality, but about partaking of the Eucharist.

> For they will be made holy who observe holy things in holiness, and those who have been taught them will find a defense.[3]

During the Byzantine Liturgy, there is a moment when the priest presents the Eucharist to the congregation and chants the words: "Holy things for the Holy." The bread and wine and Body and Blood of Jesus Christ are, in fact, the holy things of which we must partake. That is why it is vitally important also to understand the Old Testament requirement for a priest to serve at the altar of sacrifice. In *Leviticus*, we learn of Moses consecrating Aaron and his sons as priests. In the specific passage below, we see how oil and blood were used for anointing men to the priesthood. In this case, the anointing oil is a representation of the presence of the Holy Spirit, and the blood, of course, is the blood of the lamb, Jesus Christ.

---

2. *Eccles.* 9:7-8.
3. *Wis.* 6:10.

Then Moses took some of the anointing oil and of the blood which was on the altar, and sprinkled it upon Aaron and his garments, and also upon his sons and his sons' garments; so he consecrated Aaron and his garments, and his sons' garments with him.[4]

The wonderful part of this passage is that it anticipates the point that someone cannot simply claim himself to be a liturgical or sacramental servant of God. God Himself, through matter, form and ecclesiastical obedience, ordains the man to the presbyterate. This is the way we know what the truth is and that the truth is being preserved.

This is important because God was telling us that He would transform material goods into an invisible reality. God turned water into the matter used in Baptism, oil used in Confirmation, bread used in the Eucharist, and oil and blood for Ordination. Just like Judas, the Messalians ignored both the Old Testament prefigurations and the New Testament commands to live a sacramental life in Christ.

- GOD DEFINES AND DELIVERS THE SACRAMENTS IN THE NEW TESTAMENT

In the New Testament, we are told that the spiritual life—our very path to God—occurs through the Sacraments. Again, we will only focus on the Sacraments of initiation and Ordination. This first passage below is from *Matthew*, and the reference to Baptism could not be clearer.

And when they saw Him they worshiped Him; but some doubted. And Jesus came and said to them, "All authority in heaven and on earth has been given to me. Go therefore and make disciples of all

---

4. *Lev.* 8:30.

nations, baptizing them in the name of the Father and of the Son and of the Holy Spirit, teaching them to observe all that I have commanded you; and lo, I am with you always, to the close of the age." [5]

The next passage, from *John*, highlights the need to partake in the Eucharist.

So Jesus said to them, "Truly, truly, I say to you: unless you eat the flesh of the Son of man and drink His blood, you have no life in you; he who eats my flesh and drinks my blood has eternal life, and I will raise Him up at the last day. For my flesh is food indeed, and my blood is drink indeed. He who eats my flesh and drinks my blood abides in me, and I in him. As the living Father sent me, and I live because of the Father, so he who eats me will live because of me. This is the bread which came down from heaven, not such as the fathers ate and died; he who eats this bread will live for ever." [6]

In the first letter of *John* (and elsewhere), anointing is the sign of Confirmation. It is through this Sacrament that we receive the seal of the Holy Spirit, giving us the strength to do the will of God.

But you have been anointed by the Holy One, and you all know the truth. I wrote to you, not because you do not know the truth, but because you know it, and know that no lie is of the truth. [7]

What's particularly striking about the passage immediately above is that it comes in the midst of John's warning about protecting ourselves from the antichrists. For John, these are those people who seek to keep us from Christ with all kinds of lies, misconcep-

5. *Matt.* 28:17-20
6. *John* 6:53-58
7. *1 Jn.* 2:20-21

tions and misdirection. This is a reference to Judas and to all of the little Judases committing heresies against Jesus over time.

As heretics, the Messalians pursued a spirituality that denied the need for Sacraments and ecclesiastical obedience of any kind. Therefore, they also denied the need for ordained priests to maintain the truth and help us to access our God through the prayerful joining of form and matter in the Sacraments. It is exactly what St. Paul was referring to when he wrote to Timothy about Timothy's own ordination.

> Till I come, attend to the public reading of scripture, to preaching, to teaching. Do not neglect the gift you have, which was given you by prophetic utterance when the elders laid their hands upon you. Practice these duties, devote yourself to them, so that all may see your progress. Take heed to yourself and to your teaching; hold to that, for by so doing you will save both yourself and your hearers.[8]

The advice Paul gives here is that we need ecclesiastical discipline and that Ordination, conferred by anointing and the laying on of hands, should never be sacrificed for the incoherent, ecstatic utterances of untrained, nonordained members of their communities.

- THE MESSALIANS DENIED THE NEED FOR SACRAMENTS AND A TRADITIONAL SPIRITUAL LIFE

We have received much of our information about the Messalians through early Church Fathers such as St. John of Damascus, who mentions them in his book against heresies (*De Haeresibus liber*). Epiphanus of Salamis, the metropolitan of Constantia, spoke of the Messalians in his book titled *Panarion* ("medicine," as in spiritual medicine), which is a refutation of about eighty heresies.

---

8. *1 Tim.* 4:13-16

Also, we find the Messalians mentioned in *De voluntaria pauper-tate* ("On voluntary poverty"), a book written by Nilus of Ancyra, who was a disciple of St. John Chrysostom.

What we know from these and other writers is that the Mes-salians were known for their enthusiasm over the possibility of being possessed by the Holy Spirit. Known also as Euchites (both names being derivations of Greek and Syriac words for "praying men"), the Messalians based their beliefs on misreadings of *Prov-erbs* 6:4 ("Give your eyes no sleep and your eyelids no slumber") and *1 Thessalonians* 5:17 ("pray constantly"). Sleeplessness and constant praying were hallmarks of the community. What also distinguished them was their belief that the soul contained both a good spirit and an evil spirit and that even the humanity of Jesus contained a demon. They rejected the Sacraments, believed in their perfectability through prayer, and preached that a person could pray so much and so well that he could be possessed by the Holy Spirit and achieve immediate communication with God. They believed that an illuminated state would perfect their nature and release them from being accountable for their physical desires for sleep, food, sex and more.

This heretical sect took on the mantle of Judas by betraying God through denial of the Church and its Sacraments. Their so-lipsistic spirituality was enough, they believed, to achieve deifica-tion on their own. In a sense, they espoused a kind of spiritual Pelagianism.

The Messalians were condemned by local councils in Antioch (376), Constantinople (426), and Side (488), but it was the Ecu-menical Council of Ephesus in 431 that universally condemned the denial of ecclesiastical discipline and Sacraments as the source and sign of legitimate spirituality. As a consequence, the council condemned the Messalian *Asketikon* (their book on the ascetic life) as contrary to Christian theology and spirituality.

- ### Church Fathers Refute the Messalians, Defending Traditional Spirituality and Sacraments

The early Church Fathers defeated this heresy from two primary directions. First, they spoke out specifically against the Messalians and their spiritual practices, and secondly they confirmed the earlier and growing testimony about the need for Sacraments in the spiritual life.

Mark the Hermit, who was a pupil of St. John Chrysostom, wrote a treatise on asceticism in the fifth century titled *De lege spirituali* ("On the law of the spirit") in which he argues against Messalianism by detailing the duties and practices of monks, which include prayer, fasting and the Sacraments. Another of Mark's works, *De his putant se ex operibus iustificari* ("On those who suppose justification is from works"), also speaks of the spiritual life and rejects the Messalian position that grace is merely a mystical, ecstatic reality infused in the soul. He also confirms the efficacy of Baptism and the teaching of the Church that life is filled with temptation and sin and that prayer with the Sacraments form the core of our life-long spiritual journey.

Diadochus, bishop of Photice in Epirus, was an ascetic in the fifth century who spoke against the Messalians at the Council of Ephesus in 431. His great work, *Capita centum de perfection spirituali* ("One hundred chapters on spiritual perfection"), was a manual on the orthodox ways of spirituality, mysticism and asceticism and was heavily influenced by the writings of St. Paul and Evagrius Ponticus. In it, Diadochus explains the three theological virtues of faith, hope and love; that we are made in the image of God; that our likeness to God unfolds from the grace given to us in Baptism; that life is filled with spiritual struggles; and that the grace given in Baptism provides us freedom from the defeat of sin and evil, but it does not free us from experiencing them. He also explains how God's grace given so freely to us must be used to cooperate with His will and that this is done through virtue, charity and growth in knowledge of the Faith. Diadochus refutes the Messalian doctrine that man has an inner dualism and asserts that the kinds of personal illumination the Messalians preached would not be possible without the Church and the Sacraments. These ideas are also found in the teachings of many of the other spiritual masters such as Maximus the Confessor, John Climacus and Symeon the New Theologian.

Theodoret—the fifth-century bishop of Cyrrhus in Syria, who was also a writer and theologian—mentions the Messalians in his work on ecclesiastical history. Finally, the better known St. Athanasius in his treatise *On Sickness and Health* generally refuted the group of heresies that taught that the only truly spiritual life came from a day with continuous (literally uninterrupted) prayer.

As an example of those who wrote to confirm the already ancient doctrines around the Sacraments, St. Basil offers an explanation of Baptism in which he not only described the process itself but also images for us how by that Sacrament we die to a former life by the work of the Holy Spirit.

> This then is what it is to be born again of water and of the Spirit, the being made dead being effected in the water, while our life wrought in us through the Spirit. In three immersions, then, and with three invocations, the great mystery of baptism is performed, to the end that the type of death may be fully figured, and that by the tradition of the divine knowledge the baptized may have their souls enlightened. It follows that if there is any grace in the water, it is not of the nature of the water, but of the presence of the Spirit.[9]

---

9. On the Holy Spirit, Book 15:35. Philip Schaff, D.D., L.L.D., and Henry Wace, D.D., *eds, Basil,* vol. VIII of *Nicene and Post-Nicene Fathers of the Christian Churchs* (Grand Rapids, Michigan: WM B Eerdmans Publishing, 1904), p.22

St. Cyril of Jerusalem provided believers with a similar line of thinking as he wrote and spoke about Confirmation or chrismation and how the Holy Spirit is present in the oils used. You may recall the quote you read at the beginning of this chapter from the Old Testament that highlighted Moses' anointing Aaron and Aaron's sons with oil as part of the prayerful ritual to confer priesthood. Take note, too, how Cyril explains that the oils used in Confirmation demonstrate the sanctification being made through the real presence of the Holy Spirit.

> But beware of supposing this to be plain ointment. For as the Bread of the Eucharist, after the invocation of the Holy Spirit is mere bread no longer, but the Body of Christ, so also this holy ointment is no more simple ointment, nor (so to say) common, after invocation, but it is Christ's gift of grace, and, by the advent of the Holy Spirit, is made fit to impart His Divine Nature. Which ointment is symbolically applied to your forehead and your other senses; and while your body is anointed with the visible ointment, your soul is sanctified by the Holy and life-giving Spirit.[10]

St. John Chrysostom offers us a similar explanation of the Eucharist. In this passage, he exhorts us to pray and reflect as we witness the transformation of the bread and wine into the Body and Blood of Jesus Christ. He explains that through those gifts made holy on the altar we are handed the things of Heaven, and that those things came from the one who hung on the Cross for us. Finally, He encourages us to approach the altar with a deep sense of awe and love.

---

10. Catecheses, Book 21:3. Philip Schaff, D.D., L.L.D., and Henry Wace, D.D., eds, Cyril of Jerusalem, vol. VII of Nicene and Post-Nicene Fathers of the Christian Churchs (Grand Rapids, Michigan: WM B Eerdmans Publishing, 1904), p.150

When you see [the Body of Christ] set before you, say to yourself: "Because of this Body I am no longer earth and ashes, no longer a prisoner, but free: because of this I hope for heaven, and to receive the good things therein, immortal life, the portion of angels, converse with Christ; this Body, nailed and scourged, was more than death could stand against . . . This is even that Body, the blood-stained, the pierced, and that out of which gushed the saving fountains, the one of blood, the other of water, for all the world." . . . This Body has He given to us both to hold and to eat; a thing appropriate to intense love.[11]

Tertullian confirms the need for orthodox priests and legitimate ordinations. He accuses some of the sects known to him in the second and third centuries of trying to ordain men *and women* who were not properly formed and educated, which would have included knowledge of as much of Scripture as would have been available as well as the early Tradition. He also attacks those communities that promote these people very quickly without consideration for their orthodoxy or their fitness for the role.

Even the heretic women, how wanton are they! They who dare to teach, to dispute, to enact exorcisms, to promise cures, perchance also to baptize! Their ordinations are careless, capricious, inconsistent. At one time they place in office novices, at another men tied to the world, at another apostates from us, that they may bind them to themselves by vainglory, since they cannot by truth. Nowhere is promotion readier than in the camp of rebels, where, even to be there, is a merit. Wherefore one man is Bishop today, another tomorrow; today Deacon, who tomorrow will be Reader: today Presbyter,

---

11. Homilies on First Corinthians, Book 24:4. Philip Schaff, D.D., L.L.D., and Henry Wace, D.D., *eds, John Chrysostom,* vol. XII of *Nicene and Post-Nicene Fathers of the Christian Churchs* (Grand Rapids, Michigan: WM B Eerdmans Publishing, 1904), p.143

who tomorrow will be Layman; for even to laymen they commit the priestly offices.[12]

Although we do not choose to cover Confession, Anointing of the Sick and Matrimony here, you would find the same types of exhortation among the early Church Fathers to help the flock understand that there is no spirituality separate and apart from the Sacraments of the Church. These men and their communities worked diligently to preserve the true Faith that had been handed to them by the Apostles. What forms the center of their concern in the early Church was that too many groups, like the Messalians, were springing up all over the place claiming that *they* knew and understood the true Faith. Just like Judas, the Messalians were denying Jesus in the very things He gave us to know, love and serve Him in this life—the Sacraments.

- ### Modern Spirituality Denies the Need for Sacraments in the Spiritual Life

As we explained in the introduction, the most important modern form of this heresy is to be found in the prevailing attitude that seeks "spirituality" over "religion." This phenomenon in modern America has come to us by the confluence of three major activities. First, via the rampant individualism that waxed in the twentieth century. Secondly, it comes to us via the many so-called mainstream Protestant communities that decided to abandon traditional interpretations of Scripture and Tradition in favor of liberal, populist ideologies which they thought would grow their

---

12. The Prescription of Heretics, Chapter 41. The Rev. Alexander Roberts, D.D., and James Donaldson, LL.D., *eds, Tertullian*, vol. III of *The Ante-Nicene Fathers. Translations of the Writings of the Fathers down to A.D. 325* (New York: Charles Scribner's Sons, 1899), p. 263

numbers. We know, of course, that the opposite is true. Thirdly, this ideology comes to us via the secularism that has dominated classrooms and the media for five decades. Together these events have combined to create an American attitude toward religion (and the Church specifically) that is suspicious, antagonistic and dangerous for the spiritual heart of the believer.

We live in an era that encourages spiritual attitudes that attempt to steer us away from the true faith of the Church and in the Sacraments. One can picture the multitude of entertainers that try to preach their own home-grown spiritualities—sometimes cloaked in the form of exercise regimens, cosmetics lines and even home-decorating ideas—that supposedly furnish the participant with a refuge from the harshness of the business and political worlds on one hand and the ever-oppressive and suspicious world of religious institutions on the other.

On an opposite but equally dangerous pole, we also seem to be in an age experiencing the explosion of doomsday cults that tend to support a type of dualism that the Messalians could appreciate. Dualism at its core is a belief that the forces of good and evil are equally present in the universe, the world and within each person. The application of dualism in Messalianism is that the internal life—our very nature—is burdened with a separated soul where evil can only be eradicated by extreme measures of prayer and physical training. These philosophical underpinnings have contributed to an explosion of cults that see in the world an even battle between good and evil, a battle from which they must flee. This thinking spills over into their understanding of the human person, most notoriously in the belief that once spiritual perfection has been achieved in the self and confirmed by the community, one is no longer accountable for his carnal actions.

Whereas dualism in the examples above is about the internal battle between good and evil and the external manifestations of cleansing oneself from the horrors of the world, a third directional pole of modern Messalianism can be found in the cosmic dualism of Asian religions.[13] Buddhism, in particular, tends to view the world as a struggle between equally matched forces of good and evil. In the case of Buddhism, however, instead of finding an active sense of "training" the mind and body to fight the evil (through prayer and abandonment of the world), there is a kind of passivity that allows the person to find a type of inner peace through apathy. This form of passivity instructs the person to let go of any struggle and simply allow the cosmic forces around him to play out. For the Buddhist, the path of enlightenment is partly about an annihilation of specific personhood in favor of joining a "higher" consciousness.

This passivity can be identified with what is known as Quietism. Simply put, Quietistic thinking believes that man's perfection consists in the abandonment of self and an attempt at absorption into the Godhead (yes, even during our present life). The idea is that the mind becomes wholly inactive, which can lead to a false mysticism because there does not exist among those who practice Quietism an initially directional force, such as the Sacraments. There tends to be a craving among Quietists for a withdrawal from dependence on anything in the world, which leads the practitioner to a kind of Gnosticism wherein anything material is evil. Quietism in the Christian pantheon can be found among the Quakers. Even more important than them, however, Messalian Quietism can be found among the pantheistic tendencies of modern New Age movements such as environmentalism.

At the heart of all of these modern examples of Messalianism, there exists a sense of self-absorption that masquerades as

---

13. Messalianists were additionally confused in that, on the one hand, they were rigorists, while on the other they allowed too much personal spiritual experimentation.

absorption in God. This is why the ancient Messalians, and those in our modern day, reject corporate worship, Sacraments and communal prayer. This is why it is particularly disturbing that these kinds of Messalian tendencies can be found in Catholic parishes, retreat houses and convents across America. The advent of centering prayer techniques, programs of therapeutic spirituality (which, in some cases, involves practices like Reiki or spiritual massage), the stripping away of the symbols of faith within churches, the lack of focus on the Sacraments, syncretism in interreligious dialogue, and the general attitude of New Ageism have all infected the Church in the last four decades, creating a popular but false sense of distinction between "religion" and "spirituality" (with a preference for the latter). This has led the Christian faithful away from the the teachings of the Church, which are the source of religious truth, and from the Sacraments of the Church, which are the source of spiritual growth. This is the work of Judas in its most elemental form.

Liturgy
The Antidote to the
Judas Syndrome

BETRAYAL IS THE DARKENED HEART of the Judas Syn-drome. It is the recurring phenomenon of duplicity and treachery that has marked the history of man beginning with the fall of Lucifer, continued in the Old Testament through people like Alcimus, formed an apex in the life of Judas Iscariot, and found its adherents in the early Church. To make this point, we examined seven major doctrinal points of Christianity and the heresies that attacked them: Gnosticism-Docetism (denying that God came in the flesh), Arianism (denying Jesus is God), Pelagianism (denying man is dependent on God), Iconoclasm (denying the use of images of God in prayer), Macedonianism (denying that the Holy Spirit is God), and Origenism (denying a final judgment) and Messalianism (denying the necessity of the sacraments). Finally, we uncovered certain modern manifestations of the syndrome by pointing to Scientology, Jehovah's Witnesses, environmentalism, secularism and modernism in the Church, to name just a few. Along the way we discovered that some of the heretics intentionally objected to Church teaching and willfully sought to lead people away from the truth. In some cases, we dis-covered that the heresy was created by creative theology that went too far. Either way, we see that the end result is the same: the betrayal of God in His essence.

In examining how Scripture and the early Church Fathers defeated those heresies and heretics, we saw what it will take for us to fight the Judas Syndrome today. We must be vigilant in our watch over the creeping evil that seems never to give up its assault on the gates of Heaven. At the same time, we have learned that we might need to ask two final questions: first, whether we ourselves are ever guilty of being a little bit like Judas, and secondly, what will it take for us to overcome the Judas-like trajectory in the modern world.

As to the first question, regarding how we may be like Judas: every Sunday we attend the Liturgy where we give thanks, ask forgiveness, hear the Word of God, remember the life of Christ, offer gifts and sing the glories of God. On Monday we rush off to work or to school, run errands, go home, eat, and watch too much television. In the midst of the whirlwind of our activity, we may take the time to acknowledge that the world seems to be out of control. We may discuss economics, sports, politics, or even values, but it seems like people hardly ever take the time to discuss their *life in God*, and then decide to change their lives because of it. The fact is that too many of us either don't know or don't remember that all of life is within the continuum of salvation history and that this natural world in which we find ourselves is, in fact, a part of the reality of God.

All of us *say* we would never exchange Jesus for money, that we would never exchange His life for political purposes, that we would never allow ourselves to become possessed by the devil. Despite these admonitions, too many of us spend our days doing just that. We betray Christ by being workaholics, by not sharing our faith with co-workers, by committing even minor injustices, by voting for political candidates who do not defend life, by living beyond our means, by missing church, by not praying every day.

. . . Rather than imitating Judas we must *focus our lives on Christ* and be good examples to the rest of the world. More than that, we must remember that we are the inheritors of a glorious history, and that each of us must play our part within God's created hierarchy while we await our end.

God gave us a community—the Church—because He knew that we could not understand Him individually and on our own. He knew we needed a place to come to share with others what we had experienced about God and that we needed to discern, as a community, what He wanted from us. To do this, He knew we would need deeply spiritual men whose prayers would rise up to glorify God and defend what they had seen and heard. He knew we would need deeply articulate men who could write for us unified, intelligible definitions of what we had experienced.

This is the history of God's communication to the world, and it forms the beginning of the answer to that second final question of the book. In other words, the community of God, which is the Church, is necessary in aiding each of us believers in our journey toward God and in combating heresy as it springs up in every corner of the world.

- ### God Reaching Out to His People in the Old Testament

The Jews were the first to hear God's message to the world, and the ancient patriarchs and priests were the first to teach and to protect the community.

> "Hear, O Israel: the Lord our God is One Lord; and you shall love the Lord your God with all your heart, and with all your soul, and with all your might. And these words which I command you this day shall be upon your heart; and you shall teach them diligently to your children, and shall talk of them when you sit in your house, and when

you walk by the way, and when you lie down, and when you rise. And you shall bind them as a sign upon your hand, and they shall be as frontlets between your eyes. And you shall write them on the doorposts of your house and on your gates."[1]

Fortunately for us, they took very seriously the fact that God spoke to them; they knew they needed to pass down this faith to every generation. They wrote down what God told them to pass on, and they fought to maintain the truth against a host of enemies. They were confident in the covenant that God had made with man, confident that God Himself would protect His followers throughout the history of the world. The Jewish people taught us how to obey the one Lord because He is loyal, generous and just. They taught us that God is always with us, that His plan overrides the plans of man, and that we must prepare ourselves to be in His presence.

The Lord looks down from heaven; He sees all the sons of men; from where He sits enthroned He looks forth on all the inhabitants of the earth, He who fashions the hearts of them all, and observes all their deeds. A king is not saved by his great army; a warrior is not delivered by his great strength. The war horse is a vain hope for victory, and by its great might it cannot save. Behold, the eye of the Lord is on those who fear Him, on those who hope in His steadfast love, that He may deliver their soul from death, and keep them alive in famine. Our soul waits for the Lord; He is our help and shield. Yea, our heart is glad in Him, because we trust in His holy name. Let thy steadfast love, O Lord, be upon us, even as we hope in Thee.[2]

The Jews did their part to beat back the Judas Syndrome in their

---

1. *Deut.* 6:4-9.
2. *Ps.* 33:13-22

day by preserving the ancient faith for 3,000 years. They combated disbelief when they encountered it and were open just enough to God's continued revelation that God revealed Himself in an increasingly intimate way. Even though they were blind to the clues that God was a Trinity and that the persons of that Trinity would be forever in our lives in a unique way, their gift to us is that they gave birth to the people who would hear God's message in full. Namely, they gave us St. John the Baptist, Mary, and others who believed that God would come to us in the flesh.

- ## God's Desire for an Intimate Relationship with Man in the New Testament

There was a man sent from God, whose name was John. He came for testimony, to bear witness to the light, that all might believe through him. He was not the light, but came to bear witness to the light. The true light that enlightens every man was coming into the world. He was in the world, and the world was made through Him, yet the world knew Him not. He came to His own home, and His own people received Him not. But to all who received Him, who believed in His name, He gave power to become children of God; who were born, not of blood nor of the will of the flesh nor of the will of man, but of God. And the Word became flesh and dwelt among us, full of grace and truth; we have beheld His glory, glory as of the only Son from the Father. (John bore witness to Him, and cried, "This was He of whom I said, He who comes after me ranks before me, for He was before me.") And from His fullness have we all received, grace upon grace. For the law was given through Moses; grace and truth came through Jesus Christ. No one has ever seen God; the only Son, who is in the bosom of the Father, He has made Him known.[3]

---

3. *John* 1:6-18

By the time Jesus lived out His life, giving Himself in love, in word and in deed to the point of crucifixion, He showed us that eternal life has claimed us from death. God further showed us His eternal desire for us to join Him with the heavenly hosts in His kingdom forever by giving us a Comforter, Counselor and Advocate for the remainder of our days on earth.

> "If you love me, you will keep my commandments. And I will pray the Father, and He will give you another Counselor, to be with you for ever, even the Spirit of truth, whom the world cannot receive, because it neither sees Him nor knows Him; you know Him, for He dwells with you . . . These things I have spoken to you, while I am still with you. But the Counselor, the Holy Spirit, whom the Father will send in my name, He will teach you all things, and bring to your remembrance all that I have said to you."[4]

From that moment onward, there has been no excuse not to know God. He is present to us every day in the person of the Holy Spirit, and He is present to us as Son each time bread and wine are consecrated into His Body and Blood.

• JUDAS REVISITED IN THE REFORMATION

Sadly, along with the thread of continuity that can be found among the communities of believers from the ancient times until now, there is also the thread of betrayal through which we view Judas and others trying to steal us away from God. These are the two great reasons for the created hierarchy: to preserve the Faith and to defend it against the snares of the devil.

Think about the inheritance handed to us by the Apostles. They were the ones who knew Jesus, walking with Him and passing on what they learned from Him to others in the community. Their

---

4. *John* 14:15-17, 25-26.

disciples passed that Faith on to us, and now we can look back and see that we have been led by an unbroken line of succession from Jesus into our own dioceses today. This is how:

As each of the Apostles, who were the first bishops, was sent out to teach and to preach, communities were built around them and certain integral disciples were chosen to become priests in their charge. On top of their vital liturgical duties, it was common for the bishops and priests to teach and to exemplify a life of prayer and service. As we know, however, their lives were not confined to serving those who were committed believers. One heavy burden in their job was to confront disbelief in and around their community as we have pointed out with Docetism, Arianism, Pelagianism, Iconoclasm, Macedonianism and Origenism. These heresies represent all of the great debates about man's denial of God, his rejection of Christ, his ignorance of the Holy Spirit, his hatred for the Church and his derision at the Sacraments.

If this problem were only found among those who were unchurched or who persisted in a state of unbelief, then Christians could stand together against their enemies. But what we know from history is that the divisions among Christians themselves have kept us from confronting these heretics as a unified front. The chief example of this can be found in the Protestant Reformation, which caused the loss of certain traditional theologies and, most importantly, the loss of the Sacraments in many Christian sects. This historical event has severely undermined the true faith, the privilege of the people to share in the Body of Christ, traditional Christianity's unity and even its ability to combat heresy. That is why the Reformation itself must be counted as part of the Judas Syndrome.

Recall how Judas fell away, with many other disciples, over Jesus' teaching about the Eucharist.[5] The great sin of Luther, Cal-

---

5. *John* 6:64

vin, Zwingli and others was their denial of certain Sacraments and their ultimate rejection of the presence of Christ in the bread and wine. Not only did they separate themselves from the ancient Churches[6] but they opened the door for greater and great division in all Christendom.

• The Fathers on the Church

Sadly, those so-called reformers forgot what the Fathers taught us in the first centuries of the Church. They did not remember that God created the hierarchy of the Church in order to give us a place to learn and to keep us close to Him.

> The Apostles received the Gospel for us from the Lord Jesus Christ; Jesus Christ was sent from God. Christ, therefore is from God and the Apostles are from Christ. Both, accordingly, came in proper order by the will of God. Receiving their orders, therefore, and being filled with confidence because of the Resurrection of the Lord Jesus Christ, and confirmed in the word of God, with full assurance of the Holy Spirit, they went forth preaching the Gospel of the Kingdom of God that was about to come. Preaching, accordingly, throughout the country and the cities, they appointed their first-fruits, after testing them by the Spirit, to be bishops and deacons of those should believe.[7]

---

6. The difference between the Protestant schism and the division between the Orthodox and Catholic Churches is that the Orthodox and Catholics both maintained the ancient tradition, including apostolic succession and all of the Sacraments instituted by Christ. Protestants stripped many of the ancient doctrines from the Church and became a completely different kind of Christian entity. Furthermore, both the Catholics on the one side and the Orthodox on the other were able to maintain an internal unity that is not present in Protestantism. The best example of this is in the myriad schisms within Protestantism itself.

7. Letter to the Corinthians, Ch. 42. *Didascalia et Constitutiones Apostolorum.* Vol. I, Clement of Rome. (Paderborn, 1905), p. 30.

They forgot that the Church can only be one—one in the Body and Blood of Jesus Christ—in order to be unified in this cause for truth under the light of faith. They forgot that it is vitally important to us to be surrounded and protected by those who inherit their position from Christ the High Priest.

> Let all follow the bishop as Jesus Christ did the Father, and the priests, as you would the Apostles. Reverence the deacons as you would the command of God. Apart from the bishop, let no one perform any of the functions that pertain to the Church. Let that Eucharist be held valid which is offered by the bishop or by one to whom the bishop has committed this charge. Wherever the bishop appears, there let the people be; as wherever Jesus Christ is, there is the catholic church. It is not lawful to baptize or give communion without the consent of the bishop. On the other hand, whatever has his approval is pleasing to God. Thus, whatever is done will be safe and valid.[8]

They forgot that this sense of "safe" and "valid" is vital to the continuation of the Faith from generation to generation. While we can admit that specific people within the Church have scandalized it over the years, we can still proudly say that the ancient Eucharistic Churches have maintained the true faith since the time of Christ. That is why every generation must fight hard to seek out heresy and betrayal where it exists. From what God taught us from the beginning, through the command of Christ and the encouragement of the Holy Spirit, we are to rely on the Apostolic Church because only within that community can we know we are following truth and holiness.

---

8. Letter to the Smyrnnaeans, Ch. 8. *Didascalia et Constitutiones Apostolorum.* Vol. I, Ignatius of Antioch. (Paderborn, 1905), p. 121.

Since therefore we have such proofs, it is not necessary to seek the truth among others which it is easy to obtain from the Church; since the apostles, like a rich man [depositing his money] in a bank, lodged in her hands most copiously all things pertaining to the truth: so that every man, whoever will, can draw from her water of life. For she is the entrance to life; all others are thieves and robbers. On this account we are bound to avoid *them*, but to make choice of the things pertaining to the Church with the utmost diligence, and to lay hold of the tradition of the truth. For how stands the case? Suppose there arise a dispute relative to some important question among us, should we not have recourse to the most ancient Churches with which the apostles held constant intercourse, and learn from them what is certain and clear in regard to the present question? For how should it be if the apostles themselves had not left writings? Would it not be necessary to follow the course of the tradition which they handed down to those to whom they commit the Churches?[9]

You see, we recognize the truths made by God and illumined by the Holy Spirit codified in the ecumenical councils and kept by the bishops. We recognize that, through Scripture and this Tradition, we received the manner by which we come to know, love and worship God. Namely, we were given the Sacraments in order that we may have the opportunity to draw closer to God throughout every moment of our lives.

In the first place I want you to hold as the basic truth of this discussion that our Lord Jesus Christ, as He Himself said in the Gospel, has

---

9. Against Heresies, Bk. 3, Ch. 4. The Rev. Alexander Roberts, D.D. and James Donaldson, LL.D., *eds*, *Irenaeus*, vol. I of *The Anti-Nicene Fathers. Translations of the Writings of the Fathers down to A.D. 325.* American reprint of the Edinburgh edition. Revised and chronologically arranged with brief prefaces and occasional notes by A. Cleveland Coxe, D.D. (New York: Charles Scribner's Sons, 1899), p. 416.

subjected us to His yoke and His burden, which are light. Therefore, He has laid on the society of His new people the obligation of sacraments, very few in number, very easy of observance, most sublime in their meaning, as, for example, baptism hallowed by the name of the Trinity, Communion of His Body and His Blood, and whatever else is commended in the canonical writings, with the exception of those burdens found in the five books of Moses, which imposed on the ancient people a servitude in accord with their character and the prophetic times in which they lived. But, regarding those other observances which we keep and all the world keeps, and which do not derive from Scripture but from tradition, we are given to understand that they have been ordained or recommended to be kept by the Apostles themselves, or by plenary councils, whose authority is well founded in the Church.[10]

We recognize that these Sacraments not only preserve the truth of God but they are the very things that give us life. He who does not believe in them does not have life in him. This is the truth that has been spoken since Christ said it Himself. This is the difference between religions made by men and the one Faith ordained by God for man.

The body which is born of the holy Virgin is in truth body united with divinity, not that the body which was received up into the heavens descends, but that the bread itself and the wine are changed into God's body and blood. But if you inquire how this happens, it is enough for you to learn that it was through the Holy Spirit, just as the Lord took on Himself flesh that subsisted in Him and was born of the holy Mother of God through the Spirit. And we know nothing further save that the Word of God is true and energizes and is

---

10. Letters, No. 54. *Didascalia et Constitutiones Apostolorum*. Vol. I, Ignatius of Antioch. (Paderborn, 1905), p. 252-253.

omnipotent, but the manner of this cannot be searched out. But one can put it well thus, that just as in nature the bread by the eating and the wine and the water by the drinking are changed into the body and blood of the eater and drinker, and do not become a different body from the former one, so the bread of the table and the wine and water are supernaturally changed by the invocation and presence of the Holy Spirit into the body and blood of Christ, and are not two but one and the same . . . The bread and the wine are not merely figures of the body and blood of Christ (heaven forbid!) but the deified body of the Lord . . . [11]

Finally, we recognize that the Sacraments themselves, and the Church that lives them and gives them, manifests for mankind that he is capable of living in the divine world of God. What that means is that mankind was never intended merely to be a being of material reality, wallowing in the human world alone. Rather, this human world is also a world imbued with divinity. The Church, the Sacraments, the very life of man, was meant to be lifted up to God so that God could sanctify it for us as well as sanctify *us*, so that we could participate in His holy life.

- ## Evangelization and Liturgy, the Antidotes to Heresy

What all of this should mean to us in the present day is that Christian unity in the Sacraments is an important key to defeating the devil and his agents fighting against God and the Church. It should also make us more aware of what it will take to combat the Judas-like trajectory of the modern world. Simply put, prayer

---

11. Exposition of the Orthodox Faith, Bk. 4, Ch. 13. Philip Schaff, D.D., L.L.D., and Henry Wace, D.D., *eds, John of Damascus,* vol. IX of *Nicene and Post-Nicene Fathers of the Christian Church.* (New York: Charles Scribner's Sons, 1904), p. 83.

and Sacraments (in particular, the Eucharist) are the only things that are capable of bolstering men in their battle to defend the Faith and put heresy in its place.

Take a moment to think about what happens at liturgy: we remember God through the life of Jesus and beg the Holy Spirit to descend on us and the gifts of bread and wine. More specifically, in the Eucharistic Prayers we are reminded that we are a *community of memory* and a *community of transformation* called to receive, to offer and to share in the Body and Blood of Jesus Christ as the fount and summit of all Christian existence, thought and action. This happens through two portions of liturgy known as the *anamnesis*[12] and the *epiclesis*.[13]

The *anamnesis* of the Eucharistic Prayers reminds us that we are rooted in a specific history, that we are rooted in a person, in a time, in a place—and this is important. The epiclesis teaches us that we can be elevated toward God because God allows Himself to be present for us in the liturgy. This is an important point because we cannot simply set up random houses of worship and expect to be deified by encouraging words alone. In fact, we must be brought back to the unified birthplace of the Faith, and that is why these prayers are the vital recounting of our history, our identity, and give us our very life. In the liturgy, we get to know Christ by hearing about His life, by receiving the teaching of our priests, by offering ourselves to Him in supplication. We also do this by recounting the Last Supper, reliving His arrest, punishment and Crucifixion, as well as rejoicing in His Resurrection and Ascension into Heaven.

It is precisely in the liturgy where our humanity is opened up into the divine life and that the possibilities of our lives are revealed in all of their fullness. Think about what that means: God

---

12. A transliteration of the Greek word for "to put in mind again."
13. A transliteration of the Greek word for "invocation" of the Holy Spirit.

gave Himself, not merely in a distant or formulaic sense, but as one who inhabits us physically, through His real presence in the Eucharistic species, and spiritually, by light and by fire. In other words, what He did by coming in flesh and in spirit was to make it possible for man to become more like God.

Today we find ourselves embroiled in this Judas Syndrome, the recurring attempt to discredit the Faith by betraying the source and summit of that faith, the Triune God, who was made knowable to us by the Eternal Word made flesh and illumined for us by the Holy Spirit. Just as the Fathers combated the early heresies, we will only begin to defeat the heresies of our day by learning about the Faith, learning about the threats to it and immersing ourselves in prayer and the Sacraments.

This is the new evangelization. We must convince our fellow man that by His grace and mercy we know, with the fullness of truth, our destiny lies in a future life, while accepting the difficult task of building up the one now. The challenge then is to keep our feet firmly planted in this world while we keep our eyes fixed on the time of our own death and also on the final death of the world—after which we will enter into the glorious kingdom of the Lord.